By the same author, from Temple Lodge Press:

An Introduction to Counselling
Celebrating Festivals Around the World
Christ in the Old and New Testaments
Pictures from the Apocalypse
Understanding Death

Collected Plays
for Young and Old

Evelyn Francis Capel

TEMPLE LODGE
London

First edition 1992

© Evelyn Francis Capel

All rights reserved. No part of this publication may be reproduced in any manner whatsoever without the prior permission of Temple Lodge Press, 51 Queen Caroline Street, London W6 9QL.

The author asserts the moral right to be identified as the author of this work, under the Copyright, Designs and Patents Act, 1988.

A catalogue record for this book is available from the British Library.

ISBN 0 904693 34 1

Cover by S. Gulbekian

Typeset by DP Photosetting, Aylesbury, Bucks
Printed and bound in Great Britain by WBC Print Ltd., Mid Glamorgan

CONTENTS

Introduction		vii
Advent	The Twelve	1
Christmas	The Shepherds	10
	The Three Kings	25
Easter	The Three Maries	41
	The Apostles' Play	53
Whitsun	The Witness	65
Legends	The Swan Children	72
	The Children of Eve	82
	The Prince Who Knew No Fear	94
	The Island	101
	Cinderella in Egypt	112
	The Lad in the Goatskin	128
	What to do with the Dragon	145
The Seasons	The Offering	153
	The Butterfly	170
	Elemental Beings	180
Old Testament Stories	The Fiery Furnace	190
	Jonah	198
	The Angel, the Devil and Tobias	205
New Testament Parables	The King's Invitation	243
	The Good Samaritan	260

Collected Plays

The Bodhisattva's World Rununciation	277
St Francis Converts the Robbers	294
The Prodigal Son	317

INTRODUCTION

In the course of the Christian year events are celebrated which require a dramatic form; festivals need to be celebrated with pictures. Before the Reformation, many such plays were known in the English language. They were designed to be performed in honour of the festival by townsfolk and villagers. Old versions of such plays are still to be found. At the Reformation, sacred dramas were forbidden and such old texts as exist belong before that period.

Very recently, the custom has begun of reviving the Bible plays of the Middle Ages. But it is often advisable to compose modern plays on the same themes, which are easier to follow because the language and outlook belong to our own time.

The plays in this collection, performed many times, have proven to be of value in many situations. In them, an old tradition is being followed in a modern manner, and they therefore serve as examples of what can be done today. Anyone who feels the need for such plays can compose his or her own versions, or use those offered here.

Advent

The Christian year begins at Advent, the four weeks before Christmas, beginning on St Andrew's Day (30 November), or the Sunday nearest to it. I have used a drama, or ceremony, reflecting the twelve signs of the zodiac instead of an earthly story. The intention is to make real in the earthly world the cosmic pictures which are the origin of all human life on Earth. This drama, 'The Twelve', speaks of the cosmic origin of Man's appearance on the Earth, which can be understood as the meaning of Advent. There are other possibilities, of which this is one example. It is most necessary today, as part of our religious life, to stress that human beings originated in the world of the heavens.

Christmas and Epiphany

There are two stories about the event of Christmas in the Bible. One is in the Gospel of St Matthew; after the historical statements about the ancestry of Jesus, there follows the account of the coming of the wise men from the East. The other story is in the Gospel of St Luke where the first two chapters describe the Annunciation and the preparation for the birth of the Child, followed by the story of the shepherds. A close look at these stories will show that they are quite different from each other and it is no exaggeration to say that they are about different people. It is therefore appropriate to perform two different plays on separate occasions.

Christmas itself is the festival of the Holy Nights, beginning at midnight on 24 December and changing, on 6 January, into the festival of Epiphany. At Christmas, the story of the coming of the shepherds out of the night into the dawn at Bethlehem is the true picture. At Epiphany, the story of the coming of the wise men to greet the Child, whose birth was foretold in the stars, finds its true place. It is the season for 'The Three Kings' play. In this compilation of plays the two stories are kept separate. A different style is adopted for the play 'The Shepherds' to that of 'The Three Kings'. The plays should not be joined in a common performance. The festivals of Christmas and Epiphany follow each other and provide what might be called the whole story of Christmas. In fact, Christmas is threefold: it is prepared in Advent, through the experience of the signs of the zodiac, then is made known on Christmas night through the song to the shepherds, who then went to Bethlehem at dawn, and is carried into the rest of the year by the journey of the wise men.

Introduction

Easter and Whitsun

The stories in the Gospels tell of different Easter experiences in relation to different people. There is the story of the faithful women, who had stood at the foot of the Cross and then came on Easter morning to the tomb with the intention of caring for the dead body; they were the first to realize that the tomb was empty. The other experience was given to the apostles, who had gathered for their own protection in the upper room where the Last Supper was held; they were visited in the evening by the Risen Christ. There is a contrast between the faithful women going at dawn to the garden of the tomb and the apostles gathering in the place of sanctuary in the dark of the evening. There is likewise a contrast between those who were able to accompany Jesus Christ through the death on the Cross—the women, and John—and the apostles who had fled from the Garden of Gethsemane and met again in the place of the Last Supper. Other appearances of the Risen Christ are also recorded.

According to the Gospel of St Luke, at midday, two disciples were walking along the highroad. A stranger joined them, with whom they had a long conversation about the history of Jesus Christ. In the evening He was revealed to them in the form of the Master and not the stranger, and at night they met with other apostles in the upper room and He appeared again. In the Gospel of St Matthew, He was seen first by the women, who met an Angel. The apostles were led to a mountain in Galilee, where they were instructed in the mission to go out into the world of their time as messengers of Christianity.

The drama of Easter can be represented from two sides: from that of the three Maries, who visited at dawn the tomb in the garden, and of the apostles, who received the revelation of the Resurrection in the upper room, through the vision of Christ Himself. Both these scenes are required for a dramatic representation of the event of Easter.

What follows in the later events of Easter, the giving of the Holy Spirit and the founding of the Church, is represented in another play, 'The Witness'. In this St Paul is the central character. He became the apostle to the world after his encounter with the Risen Christ in his vision at the gate of Damascus. (As an alternative Whitsuntide play, it would be possible to represent dramatically the descent of the Holy Spirit onto the circle of faithful apostles.)

Legends

There are many stories with sacred content handed down from the past that are still valuable today. The examples given here are my choice, but readers can make a collection of their own and produce new plays.

'The Swan Children' is of Celtic origin and represents the experience of passing from a pre-Christian wisdom to that which is transformed by the message of Christianity. 'The Children of Eve' represents in a kind of parable a history of the Fall of Man. 'The Prince Who Knew No Fear' comes from the collection of the Brothers Grimm. From the wise and ancient tales of the Buddha comes the story 'The Island'. From Egyptian legends comes the original version of the story of Cinderella, where the intervention of the gods provides the drama. The play about the Dragon concerns the transformation of evil.

The Seasons

Further old themes have been reproduced in modern style for the sake of experiencing the events of the seasons. 'The Offering' fits in with the theme of 'harvesting' in late summer and autumn. The theme of birth out of death is found in 'The Butterfly'. 'Elemental Beings', a play for midsummer, is also on the theme of 'offering'.

Stories from the Old Testament

The plays given here are all to do with prophecy of the coming of the Messiah, or Christ, into the world of the Earth.

'The Fiery Furnace' is taken from the Book of Daniel, Chapter 3. It pictures the three martyrs, who refuse to worship the tyrant, thrown into the furnace to be destroyed. They are seen walking unhurt through the trial, in the company of a fourth figure without a name.

The play 'Jonah' represents the unwilling prophet to whom the sacred wisdom of prophecy was given when he was carried within the sacred fish to the place where his task was to be fulfilled.

The longest story is taken from the Book of Tobit, which belongs to the Apocrypha. The young Tobias is led on the venture of his destiny by the Archangel Raphael and encounters the demon which he must overcome to save the maiden who will become his princess.

Parables from the New Testament

Three of the New Testament parables have been transformed into dramatic representations. One, 'The King's Invitation' (St Matthew, Chapter 22), is a play for Michaelmas. It illustrates clearly the part assigned to Man in the evolution of world history. The Archangel Michael presides especially over the purpose and the struggle of mankind.

'The Good Samaritan' (St Luke, Chapter 10) is the story of compassion for the suffering on Earth. This theme appears in different forms in a tale of the Buddha and in a tale of St Francis. It is also found in the timeless story in the Gospel of St Luke, 'The Prodigal Son'.

The story of 'The Prodigal Son' is the pattern for all parables. The prodigal son represents the history of Man on Earth, the person I recognize in myself and the story of Man as understood by the Christ. It is the foremost story in the world and the one most needed to be carried in the hearts of people. It rouses manifold questions, has not yet found its ending, and unites us with the purpose of being human on the highest level. It could be represented in different form to the one produced here.

THE TWELVE

The Persons, Creatures and Entities

MOTHER EARTH
THE SUN
FLOWERS
STONES
ANIMALS
CHILDREN
REPRESENTATIVES OF SIGNS OF THE ZODIAC—
  PISCES
  ARIES
  TAURUS
  GEMINI
  CANCER
  LEO
  VIRGO
  LIBRA
  SCORPIO
  SAGITTARIUS
  CAPRICORN
  AQUARIUS
DEATH

The representatives of the signs of the zodiac move into a circle and each says his name in the following order: Aries, the Ram; Taurus, the Bull; Gemini, the Twins; Cancer, the Crab; Leo, the Lion; Virgo, the Virgin; Libra, the Scales; Scorpio, the Scorpion; Sagittarius, the Archer; Capricorn, the Goat; Aquarius, the Waterman; Pisces, the Fish. The movement in Eurythmy for each sign may also be done here.

MOTHER EARTH	Thoughts move within me, live, move, are, pondered through winter in quiet with awe. Who gave thoughts for winter contemplation? The planets singing moved, the stars in chorus sang.
SUN	Lonely Earth! Hear my loving call, feel my tender warmth at start of winter.
MOTHER EARTH	My heart opens wide at the great Sun's call.
SUN	Moving through the year my royal eye falls on every planet's course, on every constellation. In spring I turn to you to draw your thoughts to me.
MOTHER EARTH	My thoughts in living shape are hidden in my heart. Shoots spring, leaves spread, buds open wide. The stars give form and you give life.
FLOWERS (*with Eurythmy*)	Hidden in thought we are in this Mother Earth,

The Twelve

	waiting for the spring to call us forth.
SUN	I feel the gaze of eyes that follow my course as I move through the world.
MOTHER EARTH	All stones and mineral things spread out in space gaze at the stars above in constant contemplation.
STONES (*with Eurythmy*)	We lie motionless here until a force shall move us. We exist without life, while life flows around us. We behold the deeds of the stars and contemplate their light.
SUN (*to Mother Earth*)	I watch your living creatures as they move, jump, breathe, rejoicing in their strength, finding life in activity.
MOTHER EARTH	All my moving creatures feel the urge of hunger, the content of satisfaction, the surges of pain and joy.
ANIMALS (*with Eurythmy*)	Moving and jumping, lying and sleeping, hungering, pursuing, resting contented. Breath breathing, limbs moving, scents scenting, we are living in space, in surges of joy, in urges of pain.
MOTHER EARTH	Where are my human children to whom more is given than to others?

CHILDREN	We are here, Mother Earth. Tell us what we are given.
MOTHER EARTH	God made man, twelvefold He made him. Twelve are the circle of stars, the starry signs of the zodiac, from the twelve directions of which man is made.

(*She leads them to each sign in turn and the representatives of the signs declare what they have given to the human body.*)

ARIES	I have given you a head to think your thoughts.
TAURUS	I have given you a throat to speak and sing.
GEMINI	I have given you arms to work and wield.
CANCER	I have given you a breast for living breath.
LEO	I have given you a heart for life itself.
VIRGO	I have given you a stomach for food and strength.
LIBRA	I have given you hips for balance true.
SCORPIO	I have given you organs of life.
SAGITTARIUS	I have given you thighs to stand and move.
CAPRICORN	I have given you knees to bend and kneel.
AQUARIUS	I have given you legs to move and run.
PISCES	I have given you feet to walk on the Earth.
CHILDREN (*in answer*)	We give thanks to Him who built the body.

The Twelve

We give thanks to the stars who gave the members.

(*Then the Sun leads them again to the circle of the stars.*)

SUN — Man is a living soul.
Twelve times his mind is blessed from the twelve signs in the stars.

(*He leads them in a different order.*)

ARIES — Have faith in your thinking.
LIBRA — Build upon facts.
CANCER — Handle the substance.
CAPRICORN — Live from the worlds of the spirit.
AQUARIUS — Know the spirit of the world.
LEO — Touch and experience.
PISCES — Experience the spiritual.
VIRGO — Observe and recollect.
SAGITTARIUS — Realize the unities.
GEMINI — Calculate realities.
SCORPIO — Grasp the power of forces.
TAURUS — Exercise reason.
CHILDREN — We give thanks to Him who quickens the soul.
We give thanks to the stars for streams of thought.

(*The Sun leads the children outside the circle. The representative of Scorpio leaves his place and goes round the circle on the outside. He beckons to Death, who comes from the distance. He goes round the signs, weaving in and out of them. Then he goes to the children and takes them round the circle, beginning at Aries.*)

DEATH
(*at Aries*) God gave your head and your living soul.
I have hardened brain and bones.

(*at Taurus*) God gave your throat and your living soul.
I have hardened brain and bones.

(*at Gemini*) God gave your arms and your living soul.
I have hardened brain and bones.

(*at Cancer*) God gave your breast and your living soul.
I have hardened brain and bones.

(*at Leo*) God gave your heart and your living soul.
I have hardened brain and bones.

(*at Virgo*) God gave your stomach and your living soul.
I have hardened brain and bones.

(*at Libra*) God gave your hips and your living soul.
I have hardened brain and bones.

(*at Scorpio*) God gave organs of life and your living soul.
I have hardened brain and bones.

(*at Sagittarius*) God gave your thighs and your living soul.
I have hardened brain and bones.

(*at Capricorn*) God gave your knees and your living soul.
I have hardened brain and bones.

(*at Aquarius*) God gave your legs and your living soul.
I have hardened brain and bones.

(*at Pisces*) God gave your feet and your living soul.
I have hardened brain and bones.

The Twelve

(Mother Earth gathers the children around her.)

MOTHER EARTH
What shall become of my children
held in the grip of death?

SUN
God has sent His Son,
the spirit of the Sun,
to rescue the souls of men
from the power of death.
For all mankind's sake
twelve men were called
to the circle of His apostles,
twelve on Earth
for the twelve in the heavens.

(The Sun leads the children round the circle and they say the names of the Apostles, at each sign, one name: Aries, Bartholemew; Taurus, James the Less; Gemini, Andrew; Cancer, Judas; Leo, Peter; Virgo, John; Libra, James; Scorpio, Thomas; Sagittarius, Philip; Capricorn, Matthew; Aquarius, Thaddeus; Pisces, Simon. Then the Sun and Mother Earth stand in the centre of the circle with the children behind them. Death comes towards them with a gesture of menace.)

DEATH
My power shall grow strong
to destroy the light
and threaten you all.

SUN
My power is light
to bring life out of death.
Death shall serve life.

DEATH
The power of matter is mine.

SUN
The power of spirit is mine.

(Death crosses to Mother Earth and the children.)

DEATH	I bind them to matter and they shall be mine.
SUN	In the name of Him who came from the Sun to conquer the darkness of death, I restrain you.
	(*With a powerful gesture he prevents the resistance of Death and leads him outside the circle.*)
DEATH	You will never be rid of me.
	(*The Sun puts a chain round him.*)
SUN	Your force is restrained that you may work only to serve the good.
	(*The Sun puts Death in chains behind him.*)
SUN	The spirit of the Sun henceforth shall shine on the Earth, and the living souls of men shall shine with the spirit's light.
	(*The Sun leads the children round the signs, and they all say together the words appropriate to each sign.*)
CHILDREN (*at Aries*)	I will shine in devotion.
(*at Taurus*)	I will shine in humility.
(*at Gemini*)	I will shine in endurance.
(*at Cancer*)	I will shine in selflessness.
(*at Leo*)	I will shine in compassion.
(*at Virgo*)	I will shine in courtesy.
(*at Libra*)	I will shine in contentment.

The Twelve

(*at Scorpio*)	I will shine in patience.
(*at Sagittarius*)	I will shine in discretion.
(*at Capricorn*)	I will shine in courage.
(*at Aquarius*)	I will shine in silence.
(*at Pisces*)	I will shine in greatness of heart.

(Geometrical forms in Eurythmy are now made by the twelve signs.)

MOTHER EARTH
God made man
in the image of Himself
and gave him the strength of stones,
the life of the growing things,
the power to move and to feel.
He set his head towards Heaven
and his feet on the steady Earth.
Man shall give thanks to the Sun
and to Mother Earth below.
Their creatures shall follow him
and he shall give them love.

(The Sun stands in front of the circle.)

SUN
God made man
in spirit, soul and body.
Death entered in
to destroy body and soul.
The Son came to Earth
to bind the power of Death.
The spirit shall shine in man
as the light of the spirit shines
in the stars, who gave him life.

(Concluding procession. Music.)

THE SHEPHERDS

A nativity play

The Persons, Spiritual Beings and Animals

ARCHANGELS—
  MICHAEL
  GABRIEL
  RAPHAEL
  URIEL
COMPANY OF ANGELS
MARY
JOSEPH
INNKEEPER
OX
ASS
CHIEF SHEPHERD
THREE SHEPHERDS
GROUP OF SHEPHERD BOYS

The Shepherds

A company of Angels and Archangels

ARCHANGEL MICHAEL Dear Friends, it is Christmas tide.
At Christmas everyone listens to the Angels.
In spring we listen to the birds singing.
In summer we listen to the bees humming.
In autumn we listen to the storm sounding.
But at midwinter, when Christmas comes,
the world grows quiet and our hearts listen.
We want to hear what the Angels are singing to men on Earth.
Only the quiet in heart can hear the Angels.
Noise is made by worries and troubles,
by grumbles and grouses, by anger and fear.
Let the noise die down—the Angels are coming
to tell you good tidings of peace on Earth to men of good will.
All good people are keeping Christmas;
they are waiting to hear what the Angels sing.

(*Carol:* '*O come, all ye faithful . . .*')

GABRIEL Look up and see,
how the golden door
is opened in Heaven,
that He may come through
on the beams of the star
you behold in my hand.

MICHAEL Look up and see,
now the darkness is reft
by the blade of the light,
how the demons disperse
at the flashing sword
you behold in my hand.

RAPHAEL Look up and see,
how the curtain of cloud

	is drawn back from the stars
that grace may stream down
in the healing light
that shines from the heavens.
URIEL	Look up and see
how the doorways of Heaven
stand open and wide
that the goodness of God
be revealed on the Earth
to men of good will.
MICHAEL	The first of the quiet in heart
who could listen to the Angels
was Mary.
GABRIEL
(*to Mary*)	Hail, Mary,
chosen of God
to receive His grace and
fulfil His work.
MARY	What is this I hear?
What is this I see?
GABRIEL	Mary, fear not, thou art blessed by God.
His grace shall enfold thee.
A Son shalt thou bear,
whose name shall be Jesus.
He shall also be called
'The Son of the Highest'.
MARY	How shall this be?
GABRIEL	The Holy Spirit shall come;
the power of the Highest shall
fall like a shadow upon thee.
In the Holy Child thou shalt know the Son
of God.
MARY	Behold I am the Lord's handmaiden.
May thy word be fulfilled in me.
URIEL	The will of the Lord

The Shepherds

shall wield through the world.
The power of the spirit
shall prevail in this hour.
Mary has heeded the words of the Angel.

MICHAEL
You people on Earth,
hear the good tidings.
The Father in Heaven
sends you the Son
to hallow your feeling,
to enlighten your thinking,
to kindle your will.

RAPHAEL
The Angels in Heaven
look down to the Earth.
The Son is descending
from the heights of the world
to bring healing to men.

(*Carol: 'The Holly and the Ivy'. On Earth, an innkeeper stands outside his inn.*)

INNKEEPER
Was there ever a winter so horribly cold? The best place to be is indoors by the fire. I'll fetch wood from the stable. But it's good for my trade. Travellers are willing to pay good fat prices for food and warmth at my inn. My pockets are bulging with money.

(*The innkeeper comes into the stable and sees the ox and ass.*)

INNKEEPER
Lazy creatures, you lie there and eat while the fields are frozen. Wait a little, in spring you will work hard enough. I've a mind to get rich.

(*The innkeeper goes off and the Archangel appears.*)

ANGEL
Good Ox, good Ass,
the Angels are calling

	Make your stall ready. Pile up the clean hay. We shall bring you a Child to be born in your stable. With your breath you shall warm Him.
OX AND ASS	We are listening, good Angel, to what you are telling. We will care for the Child with our breath and our love.

(*Joseph is asleep. The Archangel Gabriel goes to him.*)

GABRIEL Go to Mary, thy wife.
She has need of thy care.
By the Holy Spirit she is with child.
The Son shall be born in Bethlehem.

(*Exit Gabriel. After a pause, Joseph wakes up and goes to Mary.*)

JOSEPH Come Mary, we must take the road to Bethlehem, King David's town. There shall the Child be born. Alas, I am old and poor, but I will care for you as best I can.

(*Joseph and Mary walk around.*)

MARY Is it far to Bethlehem on this steep, rough road? My feet stumble over stones, and the wind blows chill.

JOSEPH We must travel far tonight. Take my hand and let me help you.

(*Later.*)

See how the stars appear; by their light we shall find our way.

MARY They are the eyes of Angels looking down to cheer us.

The Shepherds

JOSEPH
: Now we have climbed the hill; there are the lights of Bethlehem.

  (*Carol: 'O little town of Bethlehem'.*)

MARY
: Where shall we find shelter, and a bed for our Child?

  (*The Archangels Michael, Raphael, Uriel and Gabriel appear in front.*)

MICHAEL
: Waken, you people,
  asleep in your houses.
  Hear the footsteps
  of him who coming
  brings you tidings
  from the Son of the Highest.

RAPHAEL
: Look up, you people,
  cast down by your trouble.
  Hear the message
  of Him who coming
  tells of salvation
  drawing near to the Earth.

JOSEPH
(*to Mary*)
: Wait for me while I knock.

  (*He knocks at two doors without answer.*)

MICHAEL
: Where are the people
  who honour God?
  Where are the people
  who pity their neighbours?

  (*Joseph knocks and the innkeeper comes.*)

INNKEEPER
: Who knocks so late?

JOSEPH
: Travellers seeking shelter.

INNKEEPER
: My house is full to the roof.

JOSEPH
: We are poor folk in need.

INNKEEPER
: This is no place for the poor. I like the chink

	of coins, and their feel in my pocket.
JOSEPH	We are seeking shelter for the Child who will soon be born. Have pity on Him.
INNKEEPER	Pity? I can't afford it. I must put myself first, I can't be expected to think of those too foolish to help themselves.

(*The innkeeper shuts the door.*)

JOSEPH (*to Mary*)	The houses are full of people whose hearts are full of care. No one has made a place for our Child. No one knew that we were coming.
MICHAEL	Alas, you people, hardened in heart. You have not heard the sound of His coming. Greed shall blind you, fear shall possess you, until you waken.
RAPHAEL	Alas, you people, blinded in spirit. You have not seen the signs of His coming. Light is at hand. Grace shall be given when you awaken.
OX AND ASS	We knew that you were coming. We have made our stable ready. We have piled clean hay to make your Child a bed.
GABRIEL	Take shelter here. Ox and Ass await you. Stars and Moon will watch you. God's Angels will guard you. The Child will bring you light.
URIEL	Here is the place appointed for you. The hour has struck wherein the will of God

	shall here be done on Earth.
MARY	Here we will take our rest, here shall our Child be born, where beasts give warmth and Angels hold their watch.
JOSEPH	How poor a place, how hard the human hearts. How helpless am I, who most would wish to help.
MARY	Take comfort. See, God's creatures pity us, and He who comes will pity those who were too blind in heart to take Him in. In God's care we will sleep.
MICHAEL	The sound of His coming is heard on the Earth. The doorways of Heaven stand open and wide. Awaken, you people, at midnight He comes.
RAPHAEL	The light of His coming shall shine through the world. The glory of Heaven shall be known on the Earth. Be watchful, you people, at midnight He comes.
GABRIEL	The Father is sending the Son to the Earth. The heavens are giving salvation to men. Listen, you people, at midnight He comes.
URIEL	The hour of His coming is divinely appointed. What the Lord has ordained is fulfilled at this time. Take heed, you people, at midnight He comes.

(Carol: 'Still the night . . .' or other music. During this, a procession of all the Angels carries the Child from Heaven and gives Him to Mary. The candles are lighted on the tree.)

COMPANY OF ANGELS
(in chorus)

Down the bright ladder
from Heaven above,
we bring the gift of God,
pledge of His love.

In dark of midnight
the bright star makes known
to those who wake and watch
our coming down.

The holy Child himself,
the gift divine,
is sent to men on Earth
at Christmas time.

Glory to God in the heights and peace on Earth to men of good will.

(Carol: 'Little Jesus sweetly sleep . . .' Meanwhile, Angels rock the crib.)

MARY

This Child of whom the Angel spoke has come on Earth to do the will of God.

JOSEPH

His name shall be Jesus, the bringer of healing.

MARY

The Angels are watching and we may sleep.

OX AND ASS

We are beside Him.
Our breath will warm Him.
Our love will enfold Him.

(Mary and Joseph sleep.)

MICHAEL

Stay near the Child,
you band of Angels.
Sing of your home
in the star-filled heights,

The Shepherds

	that He left so lately. Guard Him from loneliness here in Earth's wilderness.
COMPANY OF ANGELS	Watching beside Him Angels delight to whisper of Heaven all through the night. Nothing shall harm Him where Angels are found; the cloud of God's glory shall wrap Him around.

(*Carol:* 'While shepherds watched...'
Meanwhile, three shepherds appear.)

1st SHEPHERD	Houses are dark in the town, people asleep in their beds, but we are out on the hill, watching beneath the stars.
2nd SHEPHERD	We must guard our sheep. It is cold at midnight and the wolf is prowling.
3rd SHEPHERD	The sheep sleep safe, huddled close and warm. We should rest awhile.

(*Enter the chief shepherd with a group of boys.*)

SHEPHERDS AND BOYS (*together*)	What a life the shepherds lead, chilly hillside for their bed, fire of sticks for home and hearth, sheep for fellows songs for mirth, stars for candles, Moon for clock, so the shepherds fend their flock. But when others

lie and snore
shepherds learn
at night their lore.
Angels sing
to men below.
Shepherds hear
what Angels know.

CHIEF SHEPHERD   God greet you, shepherds.

OTHERS   And God greet you.

CHIEF SHEPHERD   And how is the night?

1st SHEPHERD   It has been quiet since sunset. It will soon be midnight.

CHIEF SHEPHERD   We will sit side by side and keep warm.

(*They huddle together, then sing in chorus.*)

What a life
the shepherds lead,
huddled close
because of need.
What can cheer us
in our plight?
Food and drink
would come aright.
Pass the bottle
hand to hand,
take a drink,
then let it stand.
Here is bread
with cheese and meat,
onions too,
and nuts to eat.
Shepherds' wives
must cook and bake,
men must eat

The Shepherds

for hunger's sake.

(Eating continues, after which a jolly song is sung.)

CHIEF SHEPHERD Stop your noise, shepherds. Listen to the quiet at midnight.

1st SHEPHERD The Earth is holding her breath, listening for One who comes.

2nd SHEPHERD The stars are watching; they see further than we.

3rd SHEPHERD The prophets have warned us to watch and wait for Him, who will come to Earth from Heaven.

1st SHEPHERD He will bring light into the darkness.

2nd SHEPHERD He will bring peace into our strife.

CHIEF SHEPHERD Let us pray.

(Chorus: Psalm 23, v. 1–5. Angels and Archangels appear.)

GABRIEL Fear not, I bring you tidings of joy. A Child is born this night in the city of David. You will find Him in the stable, lying in the manger. He is your Saviour, Christ the Lord.

ANGELS *(together)* Glory to God in the heights and peace on Earth to men of good will.

1st SHEPHERD He of whom the prophets spake in here.

2nd SHEPHERD The Holy Child has been born in a stable.

3rd SHEPHERD Let us go to Bethlehem.

CHIEF SHEPHERD Come, all you shepherds, we will go together.

MICHAEL Awaken, you people,
come to the stable.

| | At midnight He came;
                  at dawn you shall see Him. |

RAPHAEL   Awaken, you people,
               come where the star
               shines over the stable
               and beckons you on.

(Michael goes in front of the shepherds till they come to the stable, where they kneel and offer gifts.)

1st SHEPHERD   O Holy Child, Thou cam'st from Heaven
               to bring God's light to our dark minds.
               We bid Thee welcome here on Earth,
               and pledge to Thee, head, heart and hands.

2nd SHEPHERD   O Holy Child, Thou cam'st from Heaven
               to bring God's light to warm our hearts.
               We bid Thee welcome here on Earth,
               and pledge to Thee, head, heart and hands.

3rd SHEPHERD   O Holy Child, Thou cam'st from Heaven
               to bring God's will to guide our ways.
               We bid Thee welcome here on Earth,
               and pledge to Thee, head, heart and hands.

CHIEF
SHEPHERD   O Holy Child, Thou cam'st from Heaven
               to bring God's image to our sight.
               We bid Thee welcome here on Earth,
               and pledge to Thee, head, heart and hands.

MARY   Shepherds, we thank you that you came
               to bid Him welcome to the Earth.
               You are the first to see and know
               that He of whom the Angel spoke is here.

1st SHEPHERD   We will tell the tidings far and wide.

2nd SHEPHERD   We shall bring joy to all we meet.

3rd SHEPHERD   We will show the way to Bethlehem.

SHEPHERDS (*together*)	What a life the shepherds lead, poor and humble, full of need. Yet the Angels brought them light, gave them news in dark of night, led them forth to where He lay, Son of Man upon the hay. Should not shepherds now rejoice with a loud and lusty voice. Simple men they yet can know highest Man on Earth below. (*Exit shepherds.*)
ANGELS AND ARCHANGELS	Glory to God in the heights and peace on Earth to men of good will. (*Carol: 'Away in a manger...' or any other.*)
GABRIEL	Listen, you people, at midnight He came. The Heavens have given salvation to men. The Father has sent you the Son to the Earth.
MICHAEL	Awaken, you people, at midnight He came. The doorways of Heaven are opened at last. The sound of His coming

	shall not cease from the Earth.
RAPHAEL	Look up, you people, at midnight He came. The Heavens have given their grace to the Earth. The Father sends healing by the hand of the Son.
URIEL	Stand upright, you people, at midnight He came. The glory of Heaven shall shine on the Earth. The Father shall speak through the mouth of the Son.
MICHAEL	At the first Christmas, the Holy Child was born in a stable. There was no house to receive Him. Each Christmas He is born in every heart that is made ready for Him. Good Friends, the Angels still call us to prepare the house for the Christ-child. This is the song when He is born:
ANGELS AND ARCHANGELS (*together*)	Glory to God in the heights and peace on Earth to men of good will. (*Carol: 'Away in a manger...' or any other.*)

THE THREE KINGS

A nativity play

The Persons and Spiritual Beings

AN ANGEL
1st KING
1st PAGE
2nd KING
2nd PAGE
3rd KING
3rd PAGE
MARY
JOSEPH
HEROD
HERALD
SOOTHSAYER
CROWD OF PEOPLE

A Christmas-tree is centre stage, having on one side a sword and on the other a staff with a star on it. To the front of the tree stands an Angel. The Angel takes the star and walks round the audience with it while a carol is sung.

ANGEL
(*proclaiming from in front of the tree*)

All kings on Earth with wisdom crowned
look eastward and behold this light,
this morning star that rises up with
new-born strength and golden might.
The midnight of the world is past:
the dawning of the light is near.

You men in darkness look to see
the sunrise of the world appear.
Your pond'ring on the starry page
lit by the Moon across the skies
has taught you what the night reveals
of Heaven's law to human eyes.
Now turn to find the star of dawn.
It beckons you to follow on.
The dayspring from on high shall bless
what you shall find beneath the Sun.

(*1st King, with page, enters and sees the star.*)

1st KING

The night's afire with golden light
as if the Sun would oust the Moon!
What is this eastern star so bright,
outshining every planet's power?
I never saw so strange a sight.
Come, page, behold with me this sign.

1st PAGE

How can a new-born star appear
when each is fixed upon its place
and must its changeless course uphold?

1st KING

It surely holds a mystery
and points to some great soul's descent,
whose birth shall change the course of
     time.

The Three Kings

	But see, it moves and seems to show the way to search its secret out. Come, let us follow where it leads.
1st PAGE	I doubt the guidance of a star.
1st KING	But we must take a royal gift. Bring gold from my best treasure store.
1st PAGE	Sire, you will give your royal gold for this uncertain quest? Waste not your treasure needlessly.
1st KING	My page, unworthy is your doubt of our great venture. Come with me. You shall be bearer of our gift and all your doubt shall vanquished be.

(*Exit 1st King and page.*)

(*Enter 2nd King with page.*)

2nd KING	What new-born star is this, so bright that midnight dazzles me like noon? And never did a star before shed gentle warmth like these gold beams. One greater than all human souls has sent His token in this star to tell of His descent to Earth to lighten all our heavy hearts. But see how it begins to move.
2nd PAGE	Your head is always in the stars, catching some wonder strange and new.
2nd KING	Leave off untimely mocking, page. The star moves on, and we must go with eyes that only look ahead. Remember how it was foretold a Saviour should be born to us. We'll greet Him with a sacred gift,

	the best of priestly frankincense.
2nd PAGE	Why start so long a pilgrimage, wise king, for so unsure an end?
2nd KING	You tempt where you should serve. Make haste and bring our gift, for we must go. Oh, golden star, lead on aright!

(*Exit 2nd King and page.*)

(*Enter 3rd King, with page.*)

3rd KING	May all the stars of Heaven speak for my direction! What is this? What are these beams of mighty strength? What is this star that shines so bright? Some great event is shown herewith which gods perform for men on Earth. The star moves on and summons me to seek the mystery it shows. Come, page, this star shall be our guide.
3rd PAGE	Let us sleep out the night, O King, 'tis time enough to start by day.
3rd KING	Our guiding star doth shine by night. It beckons on: come quickly, now. Fetch from my store a worthy gift. Fetch myrrh for Him who now from Heaven descends to bring God's healing grace.

(*The page goes, and returns without it.*)

3rd KING	You hinder me where you should help. Search boldly, and come back again.

(*The page goes, and returns with the gift.*)

3rd KING	Now follow me with might and main and you shall see our quest prove true.

(Exit 3rd King and page.)

(Enter Joseph and Mary, followed by the Angel with the star, and stand to the left of the tree. Then Herod and his herald enter and stand to the right of the tree.)

JOSEPH

Ah, Mary, we must watch this Child
with growing care from day to day,
for many look to him with hope
that he fulfil what is foretold
of a great king from David's line.

MARY

Our joy in him is mixed with dread
and fear of every passing step,
for Envy has the sharpest ears,
and Greed can peer with quickest eye.
Might ever has a heart of fear,
and Hate a hand prepared to strike.
But see, above, the golden star
that shines upon Him since His birth.
Entrust our Child to its bright care
and to this Angel's tireless guard,
and sleep awhile.

JOSEPH

'Tis time for rest. May God us keep
awake in heart by night and day.

(The Angel sings.)

MARY

This Child new sent from Heaven to Earth
sheds light into our darkened house.
His shining infancy renews
the long-lost pattern of Man's self
as first it left the hand of God,
and hope bestirs itself that once
the fallen Son of Man be born
among the Sons of God again.

(A crowd of people who are in front of the audience move round the crib and kneel. They speak and move as if in sleep, for they are present in their night-mind.)

Crowd (*in chorus*) Bringer of light, enlighten our heads.
Bearer of love, enliven our hearts.
Giver of warmth, enkindle our will.

MARY O, Angel of the star, behold
this crowd of people, sick and sad
who come each night to gaze on Him.
They are most pitiful a sight.

ANGEL They heal their sickness by His health.
They warm cold hearts before His smile.
They would revive their innocence
and with His love cast out their fear.

MARY How may this Child bring help enough
for pain and evil grown so great?
The apple taken from the tree
that fairest was in Paradise
woke Man to Good and Evil's might,
but bore a bitter harvest since.
Therefrom grew death, with hate and strife
and fearfulness and misery.

ANGEL This tree became the tree of death
and needs must bear destruction's fruit.
But look above, at Heaven's gate
the star proclaims the coming Light.
The Light descends to dawn on Earth
in human form, for Man's release,
and once upon the Tree of death
will shine with beams of love and warmth,
for healing shall be born of death
and light arise from darkness deep.
Now, behold a prophecy—
flames of promise on this tree.

The Three Kings

(The Angel lights the candles on the side of the tree near to Mary.)

CROWD
(in chorus)
Bringer of light, enkindle our heads.
Bearer of love, enliven our hearts.
Giver of warmth, enkindle our will.

JOSEPH
How is the night? What have you heard?

MARY
No sound. But look, the daybreak comes
and will its own unquiet bring.

HEROD
(to his herald)
Go, fetch my sword, and call around
my subjects, my commands to hear.

(The herald fetches the sword from the tree and walks round the audience. The crowd moves over to Herod's side. A carol could be sung here.)

HERALD
Be silent, listen and obey!
Your king, great Herod, now will speak.
He is your governor and the head
of your whole state, who at his will
commands, and leads, and can destroy.

HEROD
I am your governor and the head
of your whole state, who at my will
commands, and leads, and can destroy.
Poor mortals, what are you without
a leader greater than yourselves?
The power to choose, for good or ill,
that fruit which made you men like gods
was for your nature far too great.
Poor wretches, you became the place
where Angels with the demons fight,
and you are pulled this way and that
by your divided nature's strife.
By dark desire you are impelled,
by conscience you would evil shun,
but still, unable to stand firm,
by conflict you are quite consumed.

But you are saved at last by *me*.
Your life is ordered to my plan:
each has his duty and his place,
his peace and his security.
But all are subject to my power
and all must fear to hear me speak.
My enemies will be destroyed,
and all who doubt are enemies.

(*Enter 1st King.*)

1st KING

The golden star which led the way
has disappeared into the mist.
I cannot tell which way to turn
but in the gloom I seem to see
a city gate with towers beyond.

(*Enter 2nd King.*)

2nd KING

Now that the star has gone from sight
I am obliged to seek the way
by asking all whom I may meet.
Please tell me, Sir, where this road leads.
What are these towers within the mist?

1st KING

That question I would ask of you.

(*Enter 3rd King.*)

3rd KING

Without the star, and in the mist,
how shall I find the way? But here
are some travellers who may know.
O Sirs, a golden star has led
my steps till now to seek a Child,
a new-born King whom I would greet.
But still I cannot find the place
and cannot tell which road to take.

2nd KING

O King, well met! I, too, have seen
the star and followed it till now.
What joy to meet a brother king
whose purpose is the same as mine.

1st KING	Then you must welcome me as third. Together we will travel on. From my far land I saw the star and understood that it proclaimed the birth of an Immanuel.
3rd KING	Well met! All three together now, we may progress more speedily. As the mist rises, I can see a city. Let us ask within.
HERALD (*to Kings*)	Strangers, who bear the look of kings and wish to enter at our gate, know that you cross King Herod's land and must appear immediately to answer what he would demand. For none may here exist with us without full permit, and our stamp on papers of identity.
HEROD	O pilgrim kings, now you have reached my city of Jerusalem. Your weary travel is repaid, for this must be the end you sought. All Herod's entertainment is yours to command. Stay here a while and wonder at what I can show.
1st KING	King Herod, for your greeting, thanks. We have looked long to find this place, Jerusalem, for here we hope to find the new-born Child we seek who is of kings the holiest, whose birth was long ago foretold and now is shown by a new star. Have you already news of him?
HEROD	This prophecy is an old tale. My soothsayer will read his book and tell us more. Come, now.

(*Enter soothsayer.*)

SOOTHSAYER   In Bethlehem, King David's town,
             which in the land of Juda lies,
             this prince and governor shall be born.
             The book does not reveal the time.

HEROD   It will have been about the hour
             when first you saw this strange new star,
             and if, in truth, the prophecy
             has been fulfilled, He will be found
             in Bethlehem, the royal town.
             Pilgrim kings, go on ahead,
             and, when you have discovered Him,
             return and tell me of the place
             that I may greet and worship, too,
             this little King, born in *my* land.

1st KING   King Herod, so it shall be done.
             We will set out in haste to find
             our journey's end and hope fulfilled.
             Farewell, till we return, O King.

             (*They go off.*)

HEROD   This prophecy would well have served
             a purpose of my own. Why should
             not I be he whom all expect?
             This young Messiah must never be
             king of these people whom I rule.

             (*The crowd follows the Kings.*)

1st KING   Oh see, the golden star again,
             larger and brighter than before.

2nd KING   See how it stops above this house
             and welcomes us with its warm beams.

3rd KING   Make haste to enter; surely here our
             purpose will be satisfied.

JOSEPH   O strangers, what do you seek here?
             A little Child lies in this house,
             his mother watches over him,

	and that is all.
1st KING	We seek the Child of whom this star is token, whose spirit shines with dawning light from Heaven above.
2nd KING	We seek the Child of whom this star is token, whose spirit shines with brightest beams of love divine.
3rd KING	We seek the Child of whom this star is token, whose spirit shines with strength to do the will of God.
MARY	As you have known Him by His star and sought Him with long pilgrimage, you are most welcome as His guests. Come near, and look your fill at Him.
1st KING	We found Thee by Thy golden star, we read Thy sign with hard-won skill, we see Thee now, a little Child, new-born within our darkened world. We who have watched the Earth's day wane towards midnight, in this darkest hour we greet in Thee the birth of light, so long awaited with desire. Just as the Sun brings back his beams at turn of winter to the Earth, so for mankind the Sun is born that shall enlighten every heart. O, Son of God in Son of Man, I bring Thee gold, the gift of kings, and, with it, all the wisdom old that men have gathered ages-long. It is a token of what lives in me as thinking exercised in long endeavour to attain knowledge of self and of the world.
1st PAGE	O kingly Child beneath the star,

               beholding Thee my doubt is gone.
               Receive this gift, and hear my pledge
               to serve Thee now with all my mind.

2nd KING   O little Child, Thy golden star
               speaks of Thy greatness in the Heavens,
               but, though on Earth Thou art so small,
               we worship Thee most reverently.
               We who have watched the world grow
                   hard
               and colder in the course of time,
               who saw the hearts of men increase
               in hate and wickedness and strife,
               we greet Thy act of sacrifice,
               we greet the power of love in Thee.
               Oh, kindle in our frozen hearts
               Thy fire divine of warming love.
               O, Son of God in Son of Man,
               I bring Thee incense of the priest,
               and, with it, all the love towards God
               that always burned in hearts of men.
               It is a token of what lives
               in me as feeling dedicated
               to what shall be revealed through Thee.

2nd PAGE   O Shining One, whose holy light
               drives out the mocking from my mouth,
               receive my worship, hear my pledge
               to serve Thee now with all my heart.

3rd KING   Thy golden star has summoned us,
               and here we kneel, our quest complete,
               to worship Thee, a Child so small,
               who in Thy promise is so great.
               We who have watched the world grow old
               and seen the life of men decay
               in sickness that, increasingly,
               seizes on body and on soul,
               we hope for life new-born with Thee
               and for Thy grace divine to heal.

The Three Kings

O Son of God in Son of Man,
I bring to Thee the healer's myrrh
as sign of that eternal core
which never died in souls of men.
It is a token of what lives
in me as willing that is strong
to follow Thy life-giving will.

3rd PAGE

O Holy One, new-born from Heaven,
who bringest healing for our shame,
receive our faith, and hear my pledge
to serve Thee now with all my will.

CROWD
(*in chorus*)

We are in the darkness—give us light,
We are in the cold earth—send us love.
We are in the hand of death—bring us life.

ALL KINGS
(*together*)

We saw Thy star shine in the East
when Earth in darkest midnight lay;
now we behold Thy countenance
and share the dawn of Thy new day.
We brought Thee gifts from ages past;
we offer head, and hand, and heart.
Touch them with Thy creating power,
transform them with Thy healing art.

MARY

The spirit of this Child will bless
your gifts and your long pilgrimage.
And may the guiding star still shine
On all your further ways of life.

KINGS
(*together, as they depart*)

God keep thee, holy Child from Heaven,
to do Thy purpose here on Earth.
God keep Thy mother for her love;
God keep Thy father for his care.
God keep us all upon our way
and send this star to be our light.

MARY

This Child has surely come to Earth
to do the mighty work of God.
His guests have greeted Him as King,

	as priest and healer with their gifts. Yet sad and anxious is my heart with dread of suffering to come. All powers of darkness gather round, eager to quench His shining light.
JOSEPH	How shall we guard Him from the wrath that jealous Herod soon will feel, hearing great Kings have been his guests?
1st KING	Our purpose ended, let us rest before we travel further on.
2nd KING	Great weariness comes over me now that our hope has been fulfilled.
3rd KING	Let us refresh ourselves with sleep.
	(*The Kings sleep. After a pause, the Angel comes to them.*)
ANGEL	O pilgrim kings, the star has led your patient feet to Bethlehem, where you with earthly eyes beheld His form, who lights your hearts with hope. The star has been your faithful guide, but he of whom you asked the way, that false king in Jerusalem, is a deceiver, who intends from envy to destroy the Child. So do not take the road again by which you came, but speedily depart towards home another way. Now blessed be your going hence as God your coming hither blest. Remember what you heard in sleep, when you awake, and give it heed.
HEROD (*to herald*)	These kings, despite their promises, have not returned as I designed. But we shall seek the new-born Child

	that claims the state reserved for *me*. Go, search in Bethlehem with care. Find every child of the same age, then kill, destroy, stamp them all out that dare to be my enemies. I am their prince and governor, and all shall have their lives from *me*.
HERALD	Great Herod, your command I hear and execute it speedily. Your enemies shall be wiped out and all your people live in fear.
	(*Herod and his herald march off. Joseph and Mary rise, ready to leave.*)
JOSEPH	Come, Mary. Herod plans our harm and schemes to find our dwelling out, so we must seek another place beyond the frontiers of his might. Long shall we wander without home, but not without the hand of God to guide the Child on His life's way.
	(*Joseph, Mary and Child go off with Angel. The Kings wake.*)
1st KING	An Angel spoke to me in sleep.
2nd KING	He warned me Herod's word was false.
3rd KING	Let us depart this way in haste.
1st KING	I laid my wisdom at His feet, but more I take than I have brought. His light shines brighter in my soul with promise of what is to come.
2nd KING	I gave my love as offering, but more received than I could give. His fire shall burn within my heart more warmly still in time to come.
3rd KING	I brought my will to offer Him;

He gave me healing back again.
His strength is planted now in me
and shall bear fruit in time to come.

(*The Kings hasten away. A carol could be sung here.*)

THE THREE MARIES

The Persons and Spiritual Beings

1st MARY (Mary Magdalene)
2nd MARY (the mother of Jesus)
3rd MARY
TWO ANGELS
COMPANY OF ANGELS

The garden of the tomb, just before daybreak. First comes Mary Magdalene, walking restlessly.

1st MARY — But Lazarus rose again; shall He who called him forth Himself do less?—Ah, I have come too fast; the long night is not done. Were my companions here, we could not yet begin to tend Him with our spices.—The disasters of these days are such a weight on my heart, as these gloomy clouds are on the air.—Now the earth quakes again, as it has done continuously since that darkened noonday.—The tremors die away, but to me it seems as if the air stirred with promise. Did He not speak prophecies of Himself?

(Enter 2nd Mary, sadly, in thought.)

2nd MARY — How small our minds for grasping such great events! So much destruction as this night has seen deadens the senses with dread. Unrest is everywhere; therefore I early seek the quiet of this garden. How slowly comes the dawn.—Strange, there is one yet here before me. Why Mary! Greetings to you! How full of fear and dread this night has been. Such earthquake and darkness! Such destruction and death! The graves have opened of themselves, they say. Strange sights were seen. I think Death never showed himself so clear.

(Enter 3rd Mary, with purpose.)

3rd MARY — Oh when will this slow night be done! No longer could I wait within dark walls, yet here the dawn comes slowly. Why sisters, are you also here so soon! Then let us make a start with our sad task, though light is faint. I am much afraid we shall be hindered. Hate and bad will are around us everywhere, and each betrays his neighbour where he can. Men's souls are darkened and possessed by forces of destruction, turning their rage against Him who brought them light. Their darkness has put out the light and men themselves made midnight of the day.

1st MARY   He accepted the darkness, as if He would plumb its depths.

2nd MARY   He had authority and power, but He did not withstand His enemies.

3rd MARY   It was as if God would accept the wickedness of men.

1st MARY   Feel how the earth still shudders. This seems to me only the echo in the rocks and stones of deeper, more terrible struggles. All night long and still before that—since the hour he died—I felt these echoes also in myself of a great struggle. For it seems to me that in the very depths of Hell, the Prince of Darkness did oppose our Master. Can you believe that His departed Spirit has striven with death? Did not the prophets long foretell that Death and Hell should once be overcome? Surely the dawn of this third day should bring us hope. But see, the sky begins to lighten.

2nd MARY   This night it seemed to me that never had I seen death grown so great, destruction so let loose. In people's faces as they passed I saw the marks of death. In every human form I felt the power of death. I understood how dead thoughts clog men's minds and dull their will. Then I remembered how, when He was with us, a stream of life flowed through us in His presence. His very words were life. Such life as this cannot be swallowed up in death. Hope will come with the morning.

3rd MARY We sit by the tomb and watch for the new dawn. Nothing is there to do but this—for Him we loved and followed—to wait and watch and care for His dead body.

1st MARY He did accept the love with which I poured the ointment over His feet.

2nd MARY Our prayers make points of light in the darkness.

3rd MARY We watch by the tomb.

(*They sing a song of mourning.*)

The earth has received Him,
The winds have bewailed Him,
The clouds have wept for Him,
Laid down in the grave.

Beasts have grieved over Him,
Birds have lamented Him,
Flowers have watched round Him,
Laid down in the grave.

Our sad hearts mourn for Him,
Our cold lips pray for Him,
Our eyes shed tears for Him,
Laid down in the grave.

1st MARY Did He not say Himself: Except a grain of corn fall into the ground and die, it abideth alone, but if it die, it bringeth forth much fruit. So was His dear body laid into the Earth's open mouth. Shall

The Three Maries

2nd MARY	such seed die and not spring up again? The light grows stronger and morning is the time of hope. But see, the dark clouds gather and press the coming dawn as if to keep it back.
3rd MARY	Let us hasten at once though the dawn is still clouded and grey, lest we be hindered from our task.
1st MARY	The tomb is here but who shall roll away the stone?
2nd MARY	The stone is very great and heavy.
3rd MARY	If only the force of earthquake could remove it for us!
1st MARY (*running on ahead*)	The stone is rolled away!
2nd MARY	The tomb gapes black and empty.
3rd MARY	Who can have done this?
2nd MARY	Was it the hand of an Angel out of the earthquake?
3rd MARY	Or straining muscles of men! And were they foes or friends?
1st MARY	The stone is rolled away (*she turns her back on the tomb.*) But see, the first beam of the Sun has risen above the clouds. Turn from the tomb! The Sun has risen!
2nd MARY (*turning also*)	At last the light has dawned again. The fearful night is over. The power of darkness has set.
3rd MARY	How like a wrestler who has conquered night, the Sun comes out between dark clouds.
1st MARY	The upper air rejoices in the light. The

Sun climbs upward on his daytime path, and throws his golden beams across the clouds, till their dark sides reflect a coloured glow. His beams strike downward now to this cold Earth, which waits in shadow for the coming day.

2nd MARY   The hilltops are lit up with golden sunlight that drives the throng of shadows to the valleys. Never have I seen so bright a glow of gold on grass and leaf. The whole land shines in the dawn.

3rd MARY   The birds' first soft greeting to the Sun is now a shout of joy. Small beasts begin to run in old tracks with new life and cheer. The flowers' unfolding buds shake out their colours in greeting to the Sun.

1st MARY   Can He still lie all lifeless in the tomb?— But look, the dark tomb is itself all light!

2nd MARY   What forms and shapes appear within the glowing light! It is more than reflected sunshine!

3rd MARY   These shapes have voices and they speak to us.

(*They come nearer and kneel. Two Angels are seen.*)

1st ANGEL   He is not here.
The seed has lain
in darkest earth.
Now a new birth
bursts from the grain,
to life He is risen.

2nd ANGEL   Fear not!
Darkness and Hell
could not repel Him.
They could not quell Him,

The Three Maries

	He broke their spell,
	in light He is risen.
1st MARY	Bright beings, tell us where He has gone.
	Has He gone to the halls of Heaven, out
	of our sight?
1st ANGEL	Oh do not fear.
	The precious seed
	in earth was sown.
	Now it is grown
	and for Earth's need
	its fruit will bear.
2nd ANGEL	Oh do not fear.
	He is not far.
	The Angels bright
	see His clear light,
	as of a new star,
	shine from Earth's sphere.

(*The Angels disappear; the women remain kneeling.*)

THE THREE MARIES (*together*)

In the sorrow of night
We came here to find Him.
With the best of our spices
We came here to bind Him.
But here is the stone
From the tomb rolled away,
The long night is over
And dawned has the day.

In the joy of the morning
They spoke words of gladness.
In the glow of the sunrise
They banished our sadness.
'The tomb is left empty,
Death is undone,
Your Lord has risen
At the rise of the Sun.'

1st MARY
: If He is risen to Heaven, then I would die to find Him. If He is risen here on Earth, then let us seek in tears till we behold Him.

3rd MARY
: Shall we not run to speak with His apostles, who sit in dread and anguish? Shall we not lighten first their gloomy hearts, then spread the tidings through the flock of those that loved Him?

2nd MARY
: Let us sit here awhile and contemplate this mystery, much too great for narrow minds like ours. Let's try with prayer to roll away the stone from this dark tomb, the human mind, which may more easily grasp death and darkness than the living light of Him from death risen up.

(2nd Mary sits down. The 3rd Mary comes to urge her on.)

3rd MARY
: See how the day grows strong. Should we not bring the joy that comes with morning to still benighted hearts?

1st MARY
: I would go further to seek our risen Master. Did not those Angel-beings say His light shines to them from the Earth? Then we must seek His shining form and find again His presence. The bright light of morning is around me, the sounds of day are in my ears, all creatures feel the breath of life. Only my heart is dark, for my eyes do not see Him. I will know neither quiet nor joy till I have found Him. I will seek further in the morning light.

(1st Mary goes off alone.)

3rd MARY
: What further would she find than the

The Three Maries

2nd MARY (*rising*) — message of the Angels? Are their words not enough to turn despair to joy? Let us go soon with our tidings.

Then let us start as you wish. We can but tell them what we have seen and what we believe. Can they believe it too?

3rd MARY — Let us tell them and their hearts will flame like ours.

2nd MARY — I cannot go so fast. My limbs were made weary by mourning and sorrow. Now they cannot bear thoughts of joy following on pain.

3rd MARY — I will support you. (*Pause.*) But you still sink down. I must wait for you yet longer.

2nd MARY — See how the dawn grows strong. A new day surely begins for us—for all mankind on Earth. Since that dark hour on Calvary, to me it seemed the Earth herself must die. Only grey meaningless dawns could follow on. Men must be caught in death without escape. Now He who brought us hope has conquered Death. And I can feel the new life quickened in my weary being and in this dying Earth. The heart feels life; the mind as yet is silent, in awe before so great a mystery.

3rd MARY — The Sun's light wakes the Earth to life again. But see, bright forms appear among its beams.

(*Out of the beams of the rising Sun Angel-forms appear—that is, on the opposite side to that from which the Angels came out of the tomb.*)

COMPANY OF ANGELS
Angels descending
On beams of the Sun,

                    Join with Earth's creatures
                    In joy new begun.
                    Earthward descending
                    Drawn to His light,
                    Long have we mourned Him
                    Gone from our sight.
                    For Earth He left us,
                    We were bereaved,
                    Into Earth's darkness
                    He was received.
                    Out of Earth's darkness
                    His light is risen;
                    Rejoice Earth's creatures,
                    To you He is given.
                    Men of the weary hearts
                    Be of good cheer,
                    Himself He will show you,
                    Unto you He is near.

                    (*Exit Angels.*)

2nd MARY   The morning is so full of Angel voices singing of joy and cheer. Let us pray that we may feel His presence here on Earth.

                (*The two women kneel.*)

                O Thou Who was dead and now art risen up, shed Thy light on our dark minds.

3rd MARY   O Thou who was dead and now art risen up, pour Thy fire into our cold will.

                (*1st Mary quietly rejoins them.*)

1st MARY   O Thou who was dead and now art risen up, thanks be to Thee, who didst open the eyes of one blind heart.

                (*2nd and 3rd Maries rise, turning to 1st Mary.*)

3rd MARY   Tell us what you have seen.

1st MARY	This way and that in the garden I wandered unheeding, not looking around me, because of the tears in my eyes. Then a voice spoke and asked why I wept. Turning, I saw through my tears Him, whom I took for a gardener. But He called my name, and my dim eyes were opened to see there our Master. I knew Him and yet did not know Him. I saw Him the same and yet transformed. My eyes beheld Him and yet He was transfigured. I knew it was a mystery and yet true. Now my tears are dry and love is in my heart.
2nd MARY	Mary, my blessing be on you and the blessing of all struggling souls.
3rd MARY	Now more than ever we must bring these tidings to all who love Him.
2nd MARY	In what words shall we speak that they may understand?
1st MARY	Let us say: The tomb was empty; Angels kept the door.
2nd MARY	Let us say: The seed that died within the grave has burst to life.
3rd MARY	Let us say: Out of the darkness of death the dawn has risen.
1st MARY	And I will say: With my own eyes I have seen Him—Christ is risen.
THE THREE MARIES (*together*)	Lord of the Sun, At dawn He is risen; Out of death's hand To us He is given. Lord of the Earth In earth laid away,

To Earth He is risen
And brings the new day.
Lord of creation
He shall appear,
Beasts, stones and flowers
Welcome Him here.
Lord of mankind
Be thou our stay,
Our guide and leader
Along Earth's way.

THE APOSTLES' PLAY

The Persons

MARY MAGDALENE
THE RISEN CHRIST
APOSTLES
  THOMAS
  JOHN
  PETER
  PHILIP
  ANDREW
  JUDE
  MATTHEW
  JAMES
  and others

Thomas is alone, musing sadly in an upper room.

THOMAS: But Lazarus came forth living from the tomb. I was myself a witness to his rising; my eyes beheld him come, all swaddled up in grave clothes like an insect's chrysalis. My own hands freed his limbs and felt them warm. Today I only found an empty tomb.

(*Enter Mary Magdalene.*)

MARY: I give you the greeting of Easter: Christ is risen.

THOMAS: But I can only answer: the tomb is empty!

MARY: Thomas, lift up your heart. I saw Him risen. In the first light of the morning He stood before me and charged me with this news to all disciples.

THOMAS: I know that He lives a spirit beyond death, and sometimes mortal eyes see spirit-forms.

MARY: No, He is here; I saw Him in the garden. And since that hour I've known it in my heart, and seen His risen light through all the world.

THOMAS: I find the world still dark and spring is mocking with sunshine and fresh flowers my weary heart. I know the dead live on in our remembrance, but we are left alone.

MARY: No, no. I saw Him risen out of death. How can I show you? Look—my tears have dried. My face was once as sad as yours is now.

THOMAS	You're asking me for faith I cannot feel.
MARY	Alas, how can I show you! Alas, poor Thomas! I will call John—he's far wiser than I.

(*Exit Mary.*)

THOMAS	Why should He rise again to this sad Earth? Death is a blessed door to worlds of light. He, the most near a god I ever met, now lives a god more worthily than here. The heavenbound soul of Man is never free from earthbound cares, from hopes and fears and toils, except by death. Would that I had died with Him.

(*Enter John.*)

JOHN	I give you the greeting of Easter: Christ is risen!
THOMAS	Oh John, I've seen His cross on Golgotha; I've stooped and peered into the empty tomb. The silence and the emptiness of death are there. Is not this empty tomb a sign He left us? We should not cling to His forsaken body, but turn to look for Him in the heights of Heaven.
JOHN	Thomas, we saw Him in this very room, no dead ghost, but arrayed in form of life. We saw Him in the form of Man from which all power of death had been cast out.
THOMAS	You saw the spirit that was freed from Earth. I well believe we are not worthy to behold Him yet in the heights of Heaven. But let us stay apart and purge ourselves from earthbound joys and duties. Then death will come and stop this double life and rest this soul that's pulled by Earth

	and Heaven two ways at once—and we shall live with Him!
JOHN	Thomas, that is not so. My soul once stood among the dead and in the light of Heaven. But then He called me to return to Earth and find Him there.
THOMAS	You may remember how I answered to Him: we know not whither Thou goest, nor the way. He answered that His way was to the Father. Where shall we find the Father but in Heaven? He is gone yonder!
JOHN	He is the Son of God, the long-awaited, whom we apostles learnt to call the Christ. In Him has all foretelling been fulfilled, that spoke of His self-offering on the Cross, of three days' journey through the depths of Hell, and His uprising from the pit of death. Do you believe He saved Himself alone, and takes alone the way to Heaven again? This is not so! He is the healer of Man's fallen nature; from death He has retrieved what death had won. The body He showed to us is for mankind a living pattern, implanted in us all as seed of what Man's nature shall become. He will abide with us, till it be grown here on the Earth, and all shall be fulfilled when sons of men become the sons of God.
THOMAS	Oh John, I know your wisdom in the spirit! My inner eye is blinded by the Earth.
	(*Enter Peter.*)
PETER	Christ is risen, brothers! Oh Thomas, where were you? Stay here with us lest

The Apostles' Play 57

	you again be absent at His coming.
THOMAS	I could not bear to watch beside His Cross. My heart refused the too sharp suffering, and numbed itself. I have become unworthy to meet His Spirit.
PETER	I was the most unworthy, were that so. I, Peter, who denied Him three times over. And yet He came to find me where I hid. All overthrown with shame and sorrowing, He raised me to new manhood. Now I know His resurrection raised me to myself. I lay in death of soul; now I am risen with Him.
THOMAS	My very heart is torn in two with doubt, and still I cannot leave my questioning.
JOHN	The steadfast question will receive its answer. Knock, and however late, the door will open.
	(*Enter the other apostles.*)
APOSTLES (*together*)	Christ is risen, brothers!
PHILIP	But where have you been, Thomas?
THOMAS	At the tomb.
PHILIP	But we have seen Him risen.
APOSTLES (*in chorus*)	Burdened and numbed, Darkened with dread, We sat apart, Mourning Him dead. One of us only Stood steadfast near, His death beholding, Keeping watch there. Three days we waited, Spellbound and dumb:

With death He wrestled
Till death was undone.
Death could not hold Him.
He rose in might;
Into our darkness
He shed His light.
As we sat silent.
He was our guest,
Finding us helpless,
Leaving us blest.

PHILIP   I knew that it was He, because at once a picture in His words came to my mind: that of the corn seed buried in the ground springing to life and growing blade and ear. The form and body we once knew was gone, sunk in the grave—a new form risen up not like the old, but like a shoot of life from the old, vanished seed.

THOMAS   All your fine pictures, Philip, are no use to me—I want to know, not only just to feel.

ANDREW   I knew that it was He, because His coming quickened new power in our sick, weary selves. Never until that moment did I know what we call life is truly living death, and holds us all in bondage. We speak of this in pictures, for more was revealed than mind or thought can grasp.

THOMAS   But that dead body taken from the Cross was no picture, Andrew, but hard fact. I cannot yet forget those wounded limbs and His great pain which you have all forgotten.

JUDE   I knew that it was He, because He came where we together sat in silent prayer. He showed Himself to us who were prepared by those three years of journeying with Him, by all He taught us, by those acts we watched, and by that sacred washing of our feet. He told us that He first would come to us and show this mystery to each single heart. You too will find Him with the eye of faith.

THOMAS
You Jude, like the others, must talk of visions, precious to the elect partaking of them. But what use are visions to those who must exist in this grim outer world which had the might to nail our Master's body to the Cross, to judge, to torture and, at last, to kill?

MATTHEW
I know that it was He, because He blessed us with peace that satisfied our hungry hearts. To each of us He gave peace with himself, which broadened out to peace with all the world, and deepened to a peace profound with God. This peace has worked in us and made us whole. It is our witness that we met with Him—we, who before were scared, benumbed and sad. Oh Thomas, try to share this change with us.

THOMAS
It is true, Matthew, that you all are changed. I envy you your gladness and your faith and wish I could escape in visions, too, from the grim memory that Jew and Roman could, with their force, defeat Him unto death.

JAMES
I knew that it was He, because He breathed a holy breath into our inmost soul, bearing the Spirit that He promised us. With this new power we are sent out again to heal and preach and break His bread among the weary, sickened

THOMAS multitudes. This priestly task shall be our evidence that He is come into our midst again and will abide with us for ever more.

THOMAS I was not with you, James. What shall I do? How can I share the task without the faith?

PETER I knew that it was He, because I heard the solemn words sending us forth again as fishermen—but fishing through the world for wandering souls, who shall be gathered in, to found on Earth the living Church of Christ. We must prepare ourselves to do His bidding and waste no time in further argument.

(*To Thomas.*)

You are our fellow-worker. Stay with us in cheerful faith and leave this questioning.

THOMAS
(*angrily*) Cut out the questions, act on faith, you say! Why have I then been given a thinking mind if not to think with? How does thought begin except with questions? Is faith unthinking? No! Such easy faith I cannot wish to have, though you can now forget the Cross and tomb and turn to gladness while I fret in doubt. But Cross and tomb are facts I cannot pass. Call me materialist if you will and say I am the hinderer who stays behind from our high task. Go on in faith! Leave me behind to doubt and to despair.

(*Thomas starts to go away and is stopped by John.*)

JOHN Stop, Thomas, stay with us! He whom we

The Apostles' Play

	follow made us one, my brothers, yet each remains himself and bears his burden, of consciousness, alone. Should we not help each other? The tireless question will at last be answered.
PHILIP	How can you share experience which you missed? Oh, Thomas, listen while we try to tell what we have seen. We saw a light more shining than the Sun.
ANDREW	We saw a form stand in that light revealed.
JUDE	We saw a human form made so divine, it seemed a pattern made by God for Man.
MATTHEW	We saw His eyes like flames of fire alight.
JAMES	We saw His lips move with intent to bless.
PETER	We saw His hands in sign of blessing raised.
JOHN	We saw the grievous wounds in hands and side.
THOMAS	Alas, I am an outcast from you all, for my eyes have not seen Him.
JOHN	Thomas, take heart, for you are sent to comfort all of those multitudes who have not seen, who fret their souls with doubt and long for vision.
PHILIP	We heard no sound of His coming nor opening of door.
ANDREW	We heard how the quiet was filled with our crying for joy.
JUDE	We heard how His voice, as of old, spoke the blessing of peace.

MATTHEW	We heard how the blessing was spoken again in farewell.
JAMES	We heard how He charged us to go forth again as apostles.
PETER	We heard how He gave to the Spirit a dwelling within us.
JOHN	We heard how He bade us to work for the healing of sin.
THOMAS	You saw Him and have told me how; you heard Him and know what He said. But who touched Him? Which of you? In that same hour I will believe and know when I see in His hands the print of nails, when I put my finger into those scars, when I thrust my hand into the wounded side.
APOSTLES (*together*)	Our eyes have seen His wounded hand and side; Our ears have heard with joy His words of peace; Our hearts have felt that He is surely risen— What need was there to touch?
	(*Easter carol. Towards the end the Risen Christ appears, giving the sign of blessing.*)
RISEN CHRIST	Peace be unto you.
	(*To Thomas*)
	Stretch out your finger for here are my hands. Stretch out your hand, thrust it into my side. Let the eyes of your soul be opened at last and find within your heart the power of knowing.
THOMAS	My Lord and my God.

The Apostles' Play

RISEN CHRIST
(to Thomas)
Your eyes have seen; the power of knowing awakens in your heart. Many there are whose eyes will not have seen. How blessed are they if they still can feel the power of knowing waken from within.

(To the apostles)

Peace be unto you.

APOSTLES
(together)
Our Lord and our God.

(The Risen Christ goes out.)

APOSTLES
(together)
Thou art the Son of God, the long-awaited.
In Thee is all fulfilled that was foretold,
who made Thyself the offering on the Cross
and gave Thy bruised body to the Earth.
Thou hast descended into Death's dark realm
and for our sake hast fought with Death himself.
Now in Thy risen form Thou art revealed,
and we the living pattern have beheld
the human form divine which Thou dost wear.
Abide with us throughout all time to come
and make us sons of men the sons of God.

JOHN
(to Thomas)
Now for a fact you know that He is risen,
for eyes and ears and hands are satisfied.
Come, join us in the tasks that He has given.

THOMAS
My brothers, now at last I comprehend
that Cross and tomb are overcome indeed:
that He is risen, master over death,
and for this life on Earth our Lord again.

I too have seen, have heard, have touched,
and now at last I too can greet you all
with that same greeting that you gave to me—
Christ is risen, brothers!

(*Easter carol.*)

Lord of the Sun,
At dawn He is risen;
Out of death's hand
To us He is given.
Lord of the Earth
In earth laid away
To Earth He is risen
And brings the new day.
Lord of creation
He shall appear,
Beasts, stones and flowers
Welcome Him here.
Lord of mankind,
Be Thou our stay,
Our guide and leader
Along Earth's way.

THE WITNESS

The Persons

CHORUS (people)
AGABUS, a prophet
PAUL
A ROMAN CITIZEN
A ROMAN OFFICIAL

At the house of Philip, the evangelist, at Caesarea.

AGABUS (*taking Paul's girdle and binding his hands*)	Thus saith the Holy Spirit: So shall the Jews at Jerusalem bind the man that owneth this girdle, and shall deliver him into the hands of the Gentiles.
CHORUS (*weeping*)	Aye, aye, alas, aye, aye, alas.
PAUL	Why are you breaking my heart? I am ready to be imprisoned and even to die at Jerusalem for the name of the Lord Jesus.
CHORUS (*embracing Paul*)	The will of the Lord be done. (*At Jerusalem.*)
CHORUS	Our beloved Paul, strengthener of our hearts, messenger of Christ Himself, is again with us. Heavy hearted, we greet him. Ominous are the signs—beware. Anger moves, violent anger against Paul. Jewish hearts fear him bitterly. Christ's way is not only that of Moses. How much they would prefer it so. Paul speaks to each and every kind, proclaiming Him, the All-Saviour Himself. (*Paul stands at the gate of the Temple.*)
CHORUS OF JEWS (*violently angry*)	Men of Israel help! Cry out against the enemy. He is of our people, against the law, against this holy place, speaking and polluting it in action. Uncircumcised Greeks he invites. (*There is a clanging of gates around the Temple.*)
CHORUS OF JEWS	Death deserving, seize him now. Let him receive judgment at our hands. Holy are the hands that strike, righteous the hearts

The Witness

PAUL	Stop! Let me speak.
CHORUS OF ROMANS	What is the confusion? What do you shout? Whom do you beat? What has he done? Why do you rave and roar in anger?
CHORUS OF JEWS	Away with him, away with him.
CHORUS OF ROMANS	Will no one give us the facts? We are deaf with your roaring. Senseless are you all, and savage. Bring him into the castle.
PAUL	May I speak to them and to you?
CHORUS OF ROMANS	Who are you? Whence are you?
PAUL	I am a Jew of Tarsus, in Cilicia and a citizen of no mean city. Let me speak to the people.
CHORUS OF ROMANS	You may speak here on the castle stairs.
PAUL	Brethren and fathers, hear my defence which I make now before you. I am a Jew, born at Tarsus in Cilicia, but brought up in this city at the feet of Gamaliel, educated according to the strict manner of the law of our fathers, being ardent in God's service as you all are this day. I persecuted this movement to the death, binding and delivering to prison both men and women, as the High Priest and the whole Council of Elders bear me witness. From them I received letters to the brethren, and I journeyed to Damascus in order to take the Christians there and bring them in bonds to

that condemn.

Jerusalem to be punished.

As I made my journey and drew near to Damascus, about noon a great light from Heaven suddenly shone about me. And I fell to the ground and heard a voice saying to me, 'Saul, Saul, why do you persecute Me?' And I answered, 'Who are you, Lord?' And He said to me, 'I am Jesus of Nazareth whom you are persecuting.' Now those who were with me saw the light but did not hear the voice of the One who was speaking to me. And I said, 'What shall I do, Lord?' And the Lord said to me, 'Rise, and go into Damascus, and there you will be told all that is appointed for you to do.' And when I could not see because of the brightness of that light, I was led by the hand by those who were with me, and came into Damascus.

And one Ananias, a devout man according to the law, well spoken of by all the Jews who lived there, came and stood by me and said, 'Brother Saul, receive your sight.' And in that very hour I received my sight and saw him. And he said, 'The God of our fathers appointed you to know His will, to see the Just One and to hear His voice, for you are to be His witness and testify to all men what you have seen and heard. And now why do you wait? Rise and be baptized, and wash away your sins, calling on His name.'

When I had returned to Jerusalem and was praying in the Temple, I fell into a trance and saw Him saying to me, 'Make haste and get quickly out of Jerusalem, because they will not accept your

	testimony about Me.' And I said, 'Lord, they themselves know that in every synagogue I imprisoned and beat those who believed in Thee. And when the blood of Stephen, Thy witness, was shed, I also was standing by and approving, and keeping the garments of those who killed him.' And he said to me, 'Depart, for I will send you far away to the Gentiles.'
CHORUS OF JEWS	Away with him, rid us of him! He ought not to live. Away with him from the Earth!
CHORUS OF ROMANS	What may this uproar signify? How shall we learn the facts? With scourging shall he be examined. In pain he shall reveal all.
PAUL	Shall a Roman citizen be so misused? Shall the law be flouted?
ROMAN	Are you indeed a Roman citizen?
PAUL	I am.
ROMAN	For a large price I bought my citizenship.
PAUL	But I am a Roman citizen born.
	(*They all part in different directions. Paul sits by himself and hears a voice from an unseen source.*)
VOICE	Take courage for, as you have testified about Me at Jerusalem, so you must bear witness also at Rome.
	(*A trial before the Jews.*)
CHORUS OF JEWS	What can we believe of him, what not? Did Pharisees and Sadduccees ever agree? Is there a resurrection? Are there Angels, are there spirits of other orders? Is the

	company of Heaven real and true? Pharisees may affirm, Sadduccees must deny.
PAUL	Brothers, I am a Pharisee, a son of a Pharisee. For what am I on trial? For what? For the hope and resurrection of the dead?
PART OF CHORUS	There is nothing wrong with him. What if he did hear an Angel speak?
OTHER PART OF CHORUS	He speaks of empty spirits in vain. It is madness to claim such acquaintances.
1st PART OF CHORUS	We find nothing wrong with him.
2nd PART OF CHORUS	We find him sadly mad.

(*The two parts of the chorus shout against each other.*)

ROMAN OFFICIAL	Of what do you accuse him? Why do you speak against him? Why do you wish him to die?
PAUL	Neither against the law of the Jews nor against the Temple, nor against Caesar have I offended at all.
ROMAN OFFICIAL	Will you go to Jerusalem to be tried?
PAUL	Before Caesar's tribunal I stand. No wrong have I done to the Jews. Had I done wrong, I would not escape death. Empty indeed are the charges of the Jews. I appeal to Caesar.
ROMAN OFFICIAL	You have appealed to Caesar, to Caesar shall you go.
CHORUS	Not the Jews, but the Romans, not the priests, but the Emperor shall decide

right from wrong. Not in the holy city,
but far away in Rome shall history be
made afresh. Not the Jews of the old ways
shall give the Messiah to the world.
Where nations are melted to nothing,
where citizen outdoes the tribesman,
there shall the name of the Saviour be
carried from man to man. There shall
mankind emerge.

ROMAN   To Caesar shall you go.
OFFICIAL

THE SWAN CHILDREN

A Celtic legend, after Fiona Macleod

The Persons and Elements

THE READER
THE ELEMENTS, represented by Eurythmy
FOUR CHILDREN (later turned into swans)—
  FIONA
  AED
  FINACHRA
  CONN
AEIFA, a witch, the children's stepmother
LIR, the King, the children's father
EBRIC, a young man
ST KEMOC
LAIRGNEN, a greedy king

The Swan Children

READER	Once upon a time there were four children of an Irish king.
FIRST CHILD	Fiona is my name.
SECOND CHILD	Aed is my name.
THIRD CHILD	Finachra is my name.
FOURTH CHILD	Conn is my name.
READER	They were always happy, gay and good—so their father, Lir, loved them dearly. They had a stepmother, Aeifa, who loved them too until she became jealous and her heart darkened. Out of jealousy she became a witch and learnt a spell to cast upon them.
AEIFA	Come, children, let us go to bathe in Lake Darvra while the Sun shines warm.
FIONA	We will gladly come.
BROTHERS (*together*)	We will gladly come.

(ELEMENTS: HARMONIOUS. *Meanwhile the children go into the water.*)

AEIFA
(*bringing out her hidden wand and tapping each child on the shoulder*)

Lose your shape as human children,
Swim henceforth and fly as birds.

(*The children acquire the shape and wings of swans. They swim around for a moment. Then Fiona comes near to Aeifa.*)

FIONA   What doom has come upon us?

AEIFA   They shall be lost on Darva's gloomy water,
With other lonely birds tossed far and wide.
Never more shall Lir behold his daughter

	And never shall his sons be by his side.
FIONA	What cruel wrong you have done, Aeifa.
	In the years long ago, long ago,
	We were loved by you who now dooms us to this cruel woe,
	Who with magic wand and words
	Has changed us into birds.
	Snow-white swans to drift nigh ever more
	Homeless, sorrowful, from shore to shore.
AED	How long shall this doom be on us?
AEIFA	Three hundred years shall you white swans
	On this lonely lake abide.
	Three hundred years again shall you
	On the northern seas drift wide.
	Three hundred years again shall you
	By the western ocean dwell,
	Till with wonder and awe you hear the sound
	Of the holy Christian bell.
CHILDREN (*together*)	Oh woe, Oh woe, far we must go From our home so dear.
AEIFA	Alas, what have I done?
	One comfort I give for wrong.
	You shall keep your human speech
	And the sweet sound of your song.
	Speed hence, speed hence, O lone white swans,
	Across the wind-scattered foam.
	The wave shall be your father now,
	And the wind alone shall kiss your brow,
	And the waste shall be your home.
	Speed hence, speed hence, O lone white swans,
	Till the ringing of Christ's bell,

The Swan Children

Then at the last we shall have rest,
And God shall take you to his breast
At the ringing of Christ's bell.

(*The swans huddle together sadly and Aeifa goes away.*)

READER Soon the father of the children was looking for them, for he missed them at home. In his search he came to the lake and heard the swans singing.

CHILDREN Farewell, farewell, farewell,
Far hence we lost ones go:
Harken our knell,
Harken our woe!

Let not our memories pass,
O ye who stay behind—
Who are as the grass
And we the wind.

LIR What has become of you my children?
I know your voices but not your shape.

FIONA We are under doom from Aeifa.

READER Then the angry king fetched himself a magic wand and found Aeifa. He had the skill to turn her into a demon of the air, wailing lonely in the storm's wind for ever and a day.

LIR
(*to Aeifa, who has acquired dark wings*)
Accursed shall you be
For deed of jealousy.
In dark wind shall you wail
Through storm and gale.

(*Aeifa flies away wailing.*)

LIR
(*to the swans*)
Sweet children, here beside the lake
I with my friends will dwell.
In peace and love we will converse
Till time doth break the spell.

READER．For three hundred years, for he came of a long-lived race, the king dwelt beside the lake with his children. His friends came with him and his enemies, hearing tell of the matter, came also and were reconciled with him. On the shores of the lake they lived in peace. The winds were kind and the children sang.

CHILDREN．The bells of youth are ringing in the
    gateways of the south,
The bannerets of green are now unfurled.
Spring has risen with a laugh, a wild rose
    in her mouth,
And is singing, singing, singing,
    throughout the world.

(ELEMENTS HARMONIOUS.)

CHILDREN．The bells of youth are ringing in all the
    silent places,
The primrose and the celandine are out.
Children run a-laughing with joy upon
    their faces,
The west wind follows after with a shout.

(ELEMENTS BEGIN TO BE STORMY.)

FIONA
(*to her brothers*)

The season of joy is past,
Dear brothers, we must away.
We shall fly to the northern sea,
To the stormy waters grey.

CHILDREN．Farewell, farewell, farewell,
With breaking hearts we flee,
For none can tell
Our wild home on the sea.

For ages on the Moyle
In loneliness and pain,
Our feet shall tread no soil,

The Swan Children

Wild wind, wild wave, wild rain.

LIR
Dear children, farewell,
Our life together is past.
The hour for death comes fast.

(*The swan children fly round to the north. Lir goes off.* ELEMENTS ARE NOW STORMY.)

(*The swan children are driven apart by the storm and then find each other. They shelter together.*)

FIONA
(*comforting the others*)
Sleep, sleep, brothers dear, sleep and dream,
Nothing so sweet lies hid in all your years.
Life is a storm-swept gleam
In a rain of tears.
Why wake to a bitter hour, to sigh, to weep?
How better far to sleep,
To sleep and dream.

READER
The long years that they spent by the northern sea were hard ones for the four swans. Through the long winter, storms beat upon them, they froze with cold and were hungry. In the summer they had respite but so lonely were they, without friends, kinsmen or humankind, that the sunlight itself did not give them joy. But whereas before they had been small, delicate swan-creatures, they now grew big through battling with the storms.

(ELEMENTS STORMY.)

FIONA
(*to her brothers*)
Come, come with me westward.
Leave the cold northern sea,
For the wild isle of Glora

Our shelter shall be.

READER
On the waves of the western ocean the swans were exposed to mighty tempests, which were hard to endure in spite of their great strength. But one day, while swimming near the shore, they encountered a young man called Ebric. He was ploughing and making poetry at the same time. He heard their songs and spoke to them with joy.

FIONA
We are the children of Lir
Who were turned into swans.
Can you tell us of our father?

EBRIC
He has passed to the Isle of the West
For his life in Erin was done.
His race has died with himself
For wonder and beauty are gone.

CHILDREN (*in chorus*)
Dim face of beauty haunting all the world,
Fair face of beauty, all too fair to see,
Where the lost stars of the heavens are hurled,
There, there alone for thee
May white peace be.

EBRIC (*in answer*)
For here where all the dreams of men are whirled
Like the sear leaves of autumn to and fro
There is no place for thee in all the world
Who driftest as a star,
Beyond, afar.

READER
Ebric went home and made a poem about the speaking swans and their fate, and all the people heard it eagerly. But the swans had to leave the shore and go out into the ocean where tempests raged.

(ELEMENTS TEMPESTUOUS. *The swans crouch together until the tempest subsides.*)

FIONA
Brothers, awake and be glad
A vision of comfort to hear,
How God in great love sent His Son
Our ways on Earth to cheer.
Our doom will once be outlived,
Our hearts will cease to mourn,
By the power of Christ himself
To life we shall be reborn.

BROTHERS
Dear sister we take heart
And put our trust in God.

READER
From that hour the swans had peace. They found shelter on the island of Glora from cold and tempest. In bright weather they swam in the blue water and flew over the sea on the wind. One day the years of their doom were finished.

FIONA
Today our doom is done.

BROTHERS
Today our exile is past.
We may leave the cold seas
For the green land at last.

(*But Aeifa still waits in the air. St Kemoc appears. He kneels to pray.*)

ST KEMOC
As it was
As it is
As it shall be
Ever more.
O Thou Triune
Of Grace
With the ebb
With the flow
O Thou Triune
Of Grace!

(St Kemoc rings his bell.)

CHILDREN What is that strange sound?

FIONA It is the sound of the Christian bell,
We have dreamed of it on the seas.
It will set us free from the spell.

(The swan children gather round St Kemoc. An Easter carol is sung.)

READER The swans lived from henceforth as companions of St Kemoc. He gave them silver chains to wear in sign that they now belonged to Christ. He taught them the holy faith which they learned gladly. They had become strong through battling with seas and tempests, and now they became wise, through all that they learnt and thought. And each day they sang at the service, till a powerful king heard of them and wanted to seize them.

(A loud noise is heard; a king, Lairgnen, comes in with Aeifa behind him.)

LAIRGNEN I am king in these parts
And news of the swans I have heard.
I want them for my own,
To have as my royal birds.

ST KEMOC They belong to Christ. See their silver chains.

LAIRGNEN Now they belong to me.

(He seizes them. Their wings fall away and they become human, but old and tired. They weep. Aeifa wails.)

AEIFA Your doom is done, but mine lives on,
As woe for me, who sinned grievously.

CHILDREN Oh woe, Oh woe, again a foe

	Has done us wrong.
ST KEMOC	In the name of God, In the name of Jesus, In the name of the Spirit, I baptize you The perfect Three of power— The little drop of the Father On thy foreheads, beloved ones, The little drop of the Son On thy foreheads beloved ones, The little drop of the Spirit On thy foreheads, beloved ones, To shield you from sorrow; The little drops of the Three To fill you with their virtue.

(*The old bodies fall down dead and the souls rise up joyfully as children.*)

CHILDREN	Behold the Lightener of the stars On the crests of the clouds And the choralists of the sky Lauding Him. Coming down with acclaim From the Father above Harp and lyre of song Sounding to Him. Christ, thou refuge of my love, Why should I not raise Thy fame, Angels and saints melodious Singing to Thee.
ST KEMOC	Dear swans, farewell Till in Paradise we meet, Till in joy with holy kiss We shall one another greet.

(ELEMENTS HARMONIOUS. *The children take Aeifa into their midst. An Easter carol is sung by all.*)

THE CHILDREN OF EVE

The Persons and Spiritual Beings

ADAM
EVE
THE CHILDREN OF ADAM AND EVE—
   CAIN
   ABEL
   SETH
   ENOCH
   ZILLAH
   ADAH
   EVA
ARCHANGELS—
   GABRIEL
   URIEL

The Children of Eve

SCENE 1

Adam is digging, Eve is spinning.

ADAM (*sighing*)	Aweary, aweary am I, toiling and moiling each day at tilling the stubborn earth until it yields us food.
EVE	Aweary, aweary am I, spinning the slippery thread, weaving and sewing the stuff to cover our nakedness.
ADAM	In the Garden of Paradise we were fed by the hand of God. Now the children clamour and cry for me to find their food.
EVE	We knew no nakedness, no fear for tomorrow's need, no bodily pain nor disease, no weariness unto death.
ADAM	Yet the Lord will not forget us. He is our help in trouble. Let us pray.
	(*They kneel down.*)
ADAM AND EVE (*together*)	Show us Thy ways, O Lord, teach us Thy paths, lead us in Thy truth, for Thou art the God of our salvation.
	(*The children of Adam and Eve come running in. They pause. Eve holds out her arms to them.*)
EVE	What shall become of the children?
CAIN	I cut off a branch of the tree with my knife. It withered away.
ABEL (*whispering to Eve*)	I peeped through the gate of the Garden. Why can't we go inside?
SETH	I had a rabbit in my arms and he snatched it away (*pointing to Enoch*).

ENOCH	Your rabbit ran off the field. He would not stay with us.
ADAH	I don't know what to do or where to go, but at least I don't quarrel.
ZILLAH	My feet stumbled over the stones and my arm hurts where I fell.
EVA	I made a basket out of rushes, but it is broken already.
CHILDREN	We are all miserable. What shall we do?
EVE	How torn and dirty you are.
ADAM	How cross and tired you are.
CAIN	Why are we still shut out from the Garden of Paradise?
ABEL	You promised us often that we should go in one day.
SETH	I asked the Angel to let me in, but he refused.
ENOCH	We asked him so politely, but he just shook his head.
ADAH	We wouldn't be tired and cross if we lived in the Garden.
ZILLAH	The branches of the trees in there are loaded with fruit.
EVA	Who eats the fruit on the trees while we are hungry?
EVE	Alas! The apple that God forbade we took and ate. Ah me!
ADAM	You shall have bread to eat and milk to drink as you need, for I have worked in the fields and milked the cows in the byre.

EVE	You shall be washed and fed. When we sleep the gate will open and we will look inside.

SCENE 2

ADAM	Wake up, wake up, be quick, for I dreamed a holy dream. Come and listen.
EVE	When the dawn came over the hill I woke with a hoping heart to meet the light of day.
CAIN	I am the first to be awake.
ABEL	I dreamt of Paradise.
SETH	An Angel brought me back.
ENOCH	But he went with the daylight.
ADAH	What shall we do today?
ZILLAH	The world is so cold.
EVA	I know a game for today.
ADAM	First we must pray.
ALL (*together*)	Show us Thy ways, O Lord, teach us Thy paths, lead us in Thy truth, for Thou art the God of our salvation.
ADAM	Come and listen. I saw in my dream two Angels, great and mighty ones. Gabriel was the name of the one, Uriel was the name of his brother. Gabriel I knew well; he it was who drove us from Paradise. They talked together of us, of our sad, unhappy life, of how they would visit us and bring us help today.

EVE	No wonder I gladly woke. Visiting Angels today! Hurry up, hurry up. It is time to make things tidy and neat.
	(*The children run round tidying up and getting washed, but they get in each other's way.*)
CAIN	Get out of my way. What is the use of Angels coming?
ABEL	He pushed me so hard. Will the Angels be angry with us?
SETH	My hair is tidy enough. Will the Angels bring us gifts?
ENOCH	My face is clean enough. May I wish, when the Angels come?
ADAH	Now comb my hair please. Will the Angels want us to be good?
ZILLAH	When can I have a new dress? Will the Angels hear us pray?
EVA	It is my turn now for the comb. Will the Angels sing to us?
EVE	How clean you are at last. But now you must be good, for who knows when the Angels come.
ADAM	Only the quiet in heart can hear what the Angels say.
	(*The children start to run about.*)
CAIN	You can't catch me.
ABEL	Let me alone to be quiet.
SETH	I don't see Angels coming.
ENOCH	Not even in the far distance.
ADAH	It is too long to wait.

ZILLAH	We can't be good for so long.
EVA	Let's look in all directions
CAIN	When the Angels come I shall tell them my wishes.
SETH	Think hard, before you speak.
	(*The children stand quietly to think.*)
EVE	What grief it is to recall how I took the forbidden fruit and saw the Angel of wrath shut the gate upon Paradise.
ADAM	What grief it is to recall that the Angels were once our friends; now we fear to meet the companions whom we loved.
SETH AND EVA	They are coming! We saw them shining in the distance.
	(*Adam, Eve and the children all line up, a little frightened. The Archangels Gabriel and Uriel approach.*)
ARCHANGELS (*together*)	In the name of God we greet you.
ADAM AND EVE (*together*)	Be your coming blest in the name of the Lord.
GABRIEL	How sad are your faces.
URIEL	How discontented your eyes.
ADAM	How grieved are your hearts as a result of sin.
EVE	How great our longing for the Garden of Paradise and the company of the Angels.
CHILDREN (*wailing*)	We don't know where to go, and we don't know what to do.
GABRIEL	We heard the sound of your tears . . .

URIEL	. . . and the noise of your quarreling.
GABRIEL	We have come to help you.
URIEL	Tell us your wishes.
EVE	Alas, there are so many. All day long they have wishes.
ADAM	Tell your wishes, my children.
CHILDREN (*hanging their heads*)	We don't know what they are. Our wishes have flown away.
GABRIEL	You cannot live like this, so discontented, any longer.
URIEL	If you have forgotten your wishes, we will give you our gifts.
CHILDREN (*holding out their hands*)	Please give us the gifts that you have brought.

(*The Angels open a sack and give out tools to each child: to Cain, a hammer; to Abel, a pen; to Seth, a spade; to Enoch, a bag; to Adah, a book; to Zillah, a spoon; and to Eva some scissors.*)

CHILDREN	What can we do with these?

(*Uriel goes to each child in turn.*)

URIEL (*to Cain*)	You shall be a maker of fine things and a builder of great cities.
(*to Abel*)	You shall learn skill with words and write in fine books.
(*to Seth*)	You shall dig in the ground and be a maker of fine gardens.
(*to Enoch*)	You shall be an honest merchant, carrying goods from place to place.

(*to Adah*)	You shall know all there is to know and teach many pupils.
(*to Zillah*)	You shall preside in the kitchen and serve meals to the hungry.
(*to Eva*)	You shall be a maker of clothes, wielding the scissors and needle.
GABRIEL	There is a skill to be learnt and work to do for each of you.
CHILDREN	Thank you for the gifts you gave; now we know what to do. Now we can set to work.
URIEL	The Lord bless and keep you.
GABRIEL	The Lord give you the fruits of your labours.
EVE	Once I saw your countenance stern with the wrath of God, now it shines with compassion.
ADAM	You have visited us with mercy, blessing our existence with the gift of skill.

(*Abel goes up to the Archangels.*)

ABEL	I remember my wish! Let us go, dear Angels, just once through the gate of Paradise.
GABRIEL	One day the gate will open for you.
URIEL	When there is no coming back, you shall go through the gate.
ADAM AND EVE (*together*)	Be your going blest, in the name of the Lord.
CHILDREN	Be your coming and your going blest.
ARCHANGELS (*together*)	May the mercy of God keep you by day and by night.

(*Exit Angels.*)

SCENE 3

The children are at work.

CAIN (*hammering*)	In the city must be a church, and that I will build first.
ABEL	The first pages of the book are written. What shall be written next?
SETH	What a large patch has been dug—it is time to start sowing seeds.
ENOCH	You will find what you need in the bag, but you must pay the fair price.
ADAH	My arms are full of heavy books and my head is full of knowledge.
ZILLAH	I have baked, boiled and stewed till my pots are full of food.
EVA	Who needs new clothes today? Who wants what I have on sale?

(*Adam and Eve come in.*)

EVE	Weary with work were we, but joy has come into toil since each has his tools and craft.
ADAM	Carefree we lived in Paradise, careworn we live on the Earth. But we have become useful people. Children, how fares the work?
CAIN	I am trying to build a city, and there is none to help me.
ABEL	Writing and writing away, it is time to have a rest.

The Children of Eve

SETH	All day long I was digging and the patch looks so small.
ENOCH	Such a thankless job is mine, taking goods from place to place.
ADAH	Why is everyone so stupid when there is so much to learn?
ZILLAH	You get thanks from none though cooking is such hard work.
EVA	How lovely the clothes looked—until people began to wear them.
EVE	You began to work with a will, now you are grumbling.
ADAM	Rest and labour—rest and labour.
	(*Gabriel comes in, at first unnoticed.*)
GABRIEL	Be blest in the name of God.
ALL	The Lord bless thy coming.
GABRIEL	Does the work prosper?
CAIN	Tell someone to come and help me—it is too much.
ABEL	None of us will ever finish—it is too long.
SETH	There is too much to be done—it is too hard.
ENOCH	Let me change to another job—it is too dull.
ADAH	There is nothing to see for my work—it is too tiring.
ZILLAH	My work is done, then it starts again. It is too tiresome.
EVA	My work gets no thanks—it is too stupid.

GABRIEL	Do you wish to change tools?
CHILDREN (*arguing among themselves*)	What a lovely plan. Give me the hammer/the book/the spoon. No, I want that. You will soon wish to give up that job. What should I like to do best?
ADAM	Jack of all trades is master of none.
EVE	Now they are quarrelling again.
GABRIEL	Will you each have your tool again?
CHILDREN (*to each other*)	Please give it back to me. It is the one I can use best.
	(*Each child says the name of his tool.*)
GABRIEL	Long learning makes skill. You will each work the better for hard-learnt skill. Do you wish to help each other?
CHILDREN	How can we do that?
GABRIEL	Each shall help his neighbour before he goes to work again.
	(*Seth holds the wood for Cain to hammer. Cain opens the book for Abel. Enoch gives Seth seed from his bag, and Seth gives him flowers in return. Zillah feeds Adah. Eva gives her scarf. Adah shows them a map. The children then all take hands.*)
CHILDREN (*chanting together*)	Are you clever? So are we, show your skill and let me see.
ADAM	Unless the Lord build the house who can prosper who dwells there?
EVE	The night comes on, the work is done, and we should pray.
GABRIEL	Shall not he who works pray?

ADAM	May the Lord bless the work. Let us pray.
ALL (*in chorus*)	Plants live in the strength of the sunlight. The human bodies work in the might of the soul's light. And what is to the plant Heaven's light of the Sun is to the body of man the soul's light of the spirit.
GABRIEL	May the work be hallowed in the holy name of Him who shall bless and keep you.
ADAM AND EVE	The Lord bless thy going. (*Gabriel goes.*)
EVE	The night brings on the dark, and when we sleep we look through the gate of Paradise.
ADAM	The dawn will bring the light. We shall become again people of use on Earth.

THE PRINCE WHO KNEW NO FEAR

The Persons and Creatures

THE PRINCE
THE GIANT
THE GIANT'S BRIDE
A LION
A MAIDEN

The Prince Who Knew No Fear

The fearless prince is roaming the world, singing as he goes.

PRINCE
Heigh-ho, heigh-ho,
away I go.
Far from home
I will roam.
The world is wide,
I need no guide.
So why stay here?
I have no fear.
Up and away!
Ho-heigh, ho-heigh.

(*He stops outside the house of the giant; he rests, sees some ninepins, knocks them down.*)

GIANT (*shouting*)
With my ninepins you play!
Get out of the way.
You are naught but a midget.
With ninepins to fidget
belonging just to me
is as risky as can be.

PRINCE
Nonsense. I moved them all.
You may well be tall
but I do what I will,
see my strength and my skill.

GIANT
Such grand words you speak!
Go away then and seek
where the tree of life grows.
Bring an apple from its boughs.

PRINCE
What for? What can you do with that?

GIANT
Myself I scarcely know,
my bride will have it so.
Find the fence with no gate,
look for beasts lying in wait,
guarding the magic tree.

PRINCE	I shall get inside, believe me.
GIANT	Stretch your hand out to grasp, feel the ring's mighty clasp, magic dangerous and dreadful, head and heart must be heedful.
PRINCE	Mine is the strength, mine is the luck.

(*The prince sets off on the journey, singing his songs on the way. He enters a garden and creeps past beasts who are asleep. He goes to the tree, puts his hand through the ring and takes the apple.*)

PRINCE	Beasts left asleep, fence passed at a leap, tree growing alone, ring hanging thereon, apple clasped in my hand, victorious here I stand. Magic flows from this ring, courage it will bring. I was bold, undismayed, no one makes me afraid.

(*The lion wakes up and comes near.*)

PRINCE	Lion go back, I take my stand. What is this? You lick my hand. Are you friend or foe? Stay there. We must make the matter clear.

(*The lion licks his hand and lies beside him.*)

PRINCE	Friend, you are my lion dear, together we shall know no fear. Mine is the apple, mine the ring. Much to the giant we shall bring. Up now and on, we start at once, bringing the apple to that dunce.

(The prince and the lion go on their journey singing. They find the giant on the lookout.)

GIANT	Where is the apple?
PRINCE	In my hand. Mine is the ring you understand. Yours is the apple as is due, given by the tree to me for you.
GIANT	Joy to my bride the apple fair, life-giving gift from thee to her.
BRIDE	Friend, you have given a gift of light. Where is the ring brought from this plight?
GIANT	I go to fetch it speedily.
BRIDE	Hero you are, or seem to be.
GIANT *(to prince)*	Give me the ring that she demands.
PRINCE	No, it is not given at your command.
GIANT	Giant am I, as strong as tall, human are you, as weak as small.
PRINCE	Mine is the ring, mine is the friend. You must with me for both contend.

(The prince and giant fight. The giant cannot win; the lion helps the prince.)

GIANT	He fights so hard the little man, the ring, the lion do all they can. What can I do? My brains I rack, cleverness serves for hitting back. Whew, overheated are we two, bathe in the river just in view.

(The prince and giant bathe. The prince lays the ring on the bank with his clothing. The giant seizes the ring, but the lion roars,

chases him, and gets it back.)

PRINCE   Mine is the ring, mine is the friend.
Mine is its magic to the end.

(*The giant hides behind the tree and jumps out on the prince, knocking him senseless. The lion laments. The giant pushes the helpless prince towards the cliff. The lion growls and pulls him back.*)

GIANT   Rid of him soon will I be
because of the ring, my enemy.

(*The giant pushes the prince again.*)

GIANT   Helpless lies the little chap,
victim of a sad mishap.
That at last shall him befall,
now so useless and so small.

(*The lion growls, pulls back the dazed prince, and then pushes the giant unexpectedly. The giant goes over the cliff.*)

GIANT (*falling*)   Woe, woe, woe,
over and down I go.
Over, over and over, gone.

(*The prince is woken by the noise.*)

PRINCE   What was that? What has become of me?

(*The lion drags the prince towards some water. He falls in and then emerges cured of his wounds.*)

PRINCE   Thanks be to God for healing,
water of life revealing,
strength that from Heaven is sent,
guiding my ways with intent.
Friend of mine, lion at my side,
now and forever abide,
companion in every hard plight,

foe turned to friend, by God's might.

(*The prince and the lion set out again together, singing. They come to a castle where a maiden stands weeping.*)

MAIDEN
Ah woe, ah woe, ah woe.
What shall I do? Where shall I go?

PRINCE
What is this misery?

MAIDEN
Enchanted the castle, enchanted me.

PRINCE
What is the remedy?

MAIDEN
Fearless the hero must be
alone in the dark to remain,
withstanding the devilish game,
three nights long, not saying a word,
three nights long, by fear undeterred.

PRINCE
Fearless was I born, danger to scorn.

(*The lion growls. They enter the castle and are beset by screaming demons. The prince remains quiet though knocked about.*)

PRINCE
Distress and din, the demons are in.
Courage about, the demons are out.

(*At dawn the maiden comes to heal him with the water of life. She has been ugly, but now she begins to turn beautiful.*)

MAIDEN
Water of life to heal,
grace of God to reveal.
Fearless to face the plight,
strength put demons to flight.

(*The second night is worse than the first. Healing with water is repeated.*)

(*The third night the devilry reaches a climax. The prince is annointed with the water of life and the maiden's words are repeated. She turns even more beautiful and the castle begins to shine.*)

MAIDEN

Three nights long not saying a word,
three nights long by fear undeterred,
hero worthy of due reward.
Princess to wife, kingdom to guard.
welcome within to all that is mine.
Welcome to lion in friendship so fine.
He never in trouble left you alone,
he never in sorrow let out a moan.
Welcome to hero so steadfast in pluck,
sorrow is over, forgotten in luck.

(*The lion joins the hands of the prince and the maiden. He has now become able to speak.*)

LION

Princess is Queen, Prince becomes King.
Demons are done for,
let the bells ring!
Let the dance start, let the songs sound.
Let friend, let lover meet in the round.
Fear is put out, courage shall shine,
gift from the lion to your heart and mine.

(*Song.*)

Lion of the golden eyes, make me wise.
Lion of the valorous heart, take my part.
Lion of the Sun, shining bright, impart
   your light.
Lion of sure faith, true to the end, be my
   friend.

THE ISLAND

The play is based on one of the tales told by the Buddha to his disciples. It opens with a shipwreck in which the anxiety of the sailors is the theme, and is a parable for the miseries and uncertainties of our present times.

The Persons, Spiritual Beings and Entities

SEVEN SAILORS (one more wakeful than the others)
A WAVE
GOBLINS IN THE GUISE OF WOMEN
UNICORN
THE ARCHANGEL MICHAEL

Sailors are clinging to a ship that is capsizing in a stormy sea.

SAILORS	Ai . . . ai . . . ay . . . ee . . . ee . . . oh woe! The end is near, full of fear, Waves beat with dread about our head. Where shall we go, tossed to and fro, By the dangers of life, by the terrors of strife. Sleeping in spite, waking in woe, Living is dire and dying is doom.
WAVE	They are not brave, they fear the wave, They hold not course, the woe is worse.
SAILORS	We are not brave, we dread each wave, Each load to bear of heavy care. We slide and slip, we take no grip, We let things slide upon the tide.
WAVE	If they were brave, meeting the wave, We would uphold their struggle bold.
SAILORS	We drown in fear, though help is near. What shall we do for courage true? Where is the aim, where is the fame? Our strength to sustain, faith to inflame.
WAVE (*to sailors*)	Look up beyond, I say to you, Go down in fear, rise up in hope.
SAILORS (*each in turn*)	What are we doing? Someone should save us. What is the cost? We might fail. Let's be safe at all costs. Who will save us?
WAVE	Float with me, upon my wave, Float away to the new day.
SAILORS	Trust in the tide with the waves to abide, To be swept to an isle to dwell there for a while

The Island

Gives us respite from Woe. To land we
    will go.
Thrown about in the storm, we come to
    much harm.
Jolted hither and thither.
To ourselves we are lost, to circumstance
    tossed,
Lost souls shall we be in the wide world
    at sea.

WAVE
Float to shore, upon my back,
Rest at ease while in my power.

(*Goblins in the guise of beautiful women call from an island.*)

GOBLIN WOMEN (*calling to the sailors*)
Hey, hey,
Leave the waves,
Leave the tide,
Leave the storm,
Take refuge here.

Leave the struggle,
Leave the stress,
Leave the strain,
Find rest with us.

Accept the calm,
Accept the comfort,
Accept the kisses
Of consolation.

(*The goblin women receive the sailors on the shore with embraces.*)

SAILORS
Wonder of wonders!
The soundness of ground underfoot,
The sweetness of scent from the earth,
The firmness of touch on the stone,
The greenness of grass and of leaves,
The fragrance of flowers in the field,
The singing of birds in the trees,

	The footfalls of animal feet,
	They weave in the magic of wonder
	Round the hearts of those who roamed
	Over rolling waves too long.
GOBLIN WOMEN	We welcome the wanderers
	Who are washed up among us
	From the boundless waves of dread.
	We pull them towards us
	To warm them from cold,
	To console them from fear,
	To release from the dread,
	Changing comfort for woe.
	We await you with longing
	On this island of women
	Whence the men-folk went forth
	long ages ago.
	Come to caresses
	heartfelt and warm,
	Come to the pitying arms
	That will melt the sad harm
	Wrought by much trouble
	That hearts may be glowing
	And lips may be singing.

(*The sailors and goblin women embrace.*)

SAILORS The power of God has brought us here.
Head, heart and hand shall praise Him.

GOBLIN WOMEN (*to sailors*) You have been given to us.

(*To each other.*)

Goblins, go-getters, are we,
Enjoying with our goblin glee
Mortals lured to come our way
Confusedly tempted astray
By the wicked wiles we work
On the wishes that do lurk
In the caverns of the heart.

The Island

Soothing sweet sisters are we,
Submerging in dreamtime the souls
Of those who submit to our sway
Who happily follow our way
Ceasing to hope,
Rejecting despair,
Letting go effort,
Relinquishing care
Till they float in the mist of our weaving.

SAILORS
(each in turn)

We can relax now.
It's no good looking ahead.
After all, we deserve a rest.
It's a bit of luck to be here.
Why worry?
It's all for the best.
Praise the Lord.

(*The goblin women wrap up the sailors and lay them to rest.*)

GOBLIN WOMEN

Sleep your sleep out,
There is rest for the weary.

(*The goblin women sing a lullaby.*)

Lay aside care,
Throw away fear,
Dreams shall enfold you,
Sleep shall uphold you,
We will watch round you
Till dreams come true.

(*The goblin women do the goblins' dance and fasten chains of flowers on the sleeping sailors. After a pause, the sailors wake up.*)

SAILORS
(each in turn)

What a dream!
If my dream were true, how happy I would be.
Everything I ever wanted.
Such bliss to be here.

	Are we really awake? When will it end? Let's enjoy it while it lasts.
GOBLIN WOMEN	Lovely moments, happy hours, Wake to wonders, Rest in bowers, Come and join the magic dance.
	(*The women pull the sailors by the chains into the goblin dance.*)
GOBLIN WOMEN (*chanting*)	Swing and swirl, Weave and whirl, Hold your hands, Join in bands, Break the ring, Begin to sing, Twirl around, Foot the sound, Find your place, Keep up the pace. Twirling, whirling, Hurling, swirling.
SAILORS (*singing*)	Happy as the day is long, Sweet the dance and bold the song. Once we sailed the sea in dread, Now on softest lawns we tread.
	(*A great meal is laid out and each sailor is guided to it by the chain.*)
GOBLIN WOMEN	No more starving, No more craving, No more dreading, No more grieving. Happy eaters, Jolly diners, Eager drinkers Make fine suitors.

SAILORS	Pass my plate, fill my cup, Send them round to the sound Of happy chewing, hearty drinking. More, more, give us more, Much, much, let's take too much.
GOBLIN WOMEN	They shout for more Who soon will snore. With hunger sad, With surfeit glad, They're tossed to and fro' Between joy and woe. They will eat from our hands And be pulled by our bands.
SAILORS	Generous ladies, generous still, Let us eat and drink our fill.
GOBLIN WOMEN	Come and take, Hunger fades for eating's sake.

(*The sailors fall over in a stupor, one by one. One sailor stays awake longer.*)

WAKEFUL SAILOR	Hunger is hateful But greed is baleful. Greedy beyond belief, Sleep will bring relief.

(*The women dance the goblin dance, chanting the verse again, Goblins, go-getters, are we . . . The wakeful sailor listens and the women dance away.*)

WAKEFUL SAILOR	Generous ladies, generous still Why do they care for us so well? Do they pity us, or hate? Are they offering gifts, or bait? Are they good, or are they evil? Do they serve God, or the Devil?

(*The wakeful sailor discovers that he is wearing a chain.*)

How comes the chain to bind my hand,
Have I been pulled at their command?
My comrades too are bound with chains,
Are we enslaved to goblin games?

(*He goes round shaking the sailors awake.*)

Awake, awake, for danger's sake!
Enthralled by dreams, what kindness seems
Is but deception and evil intention.
Discover your chains tied to evil aims.
They are goblins all, these ladies tall.
They dance your doom, it comes so soon.
No one can fly while they are by.
To evil ends they have tied our hands.
They are foes hid in friends and friends as foes.

SAILORS
(*awakened*)

They are friendly enough.
They rescued us from the sea.
I have never been so comfortable before.
I can see the chains, but why?
Are we bewitched?
Are we playing the Devil's game?
How can we get out of here?

WAKEFUL
SAILOR

The grip of goblins holds us tight.
They make us slaves held in their might.
So wrapped in pleasant dreams are we,
Our human minds have ceased to be.
Our senses gone, our conscience fled,
Our will to devilry is fed.

ANOTHER
SAILOR

It is pleasant enough devilry.
I have never known such comfort.

WAKEFUL
SAILOR

Is there no escape from the chain?
Are we dreaming away our existence?
How can I be human again?
O Lord, be our present help in trouble.

The Island

(There is a flash of lightning, and a unicorn appears.)

UNICORN
From clouds of light
I saw your plight.
On waves of fear
In deep despair
The dark devil of gloom
pushed you to doom.
The light devil saved you,
In comfort enslaved you,
Pulls you on chains
with devilish claims.
Stop and awake
For your true spirit's sake.
Rise with me to clear light.

WAKEFUL SAILOR
Take me with you.
On the white wings of wisdom
I will rise up with you.

ANOTHER SAILOR
Take me with you to the realms of God.
I would escape from both devils.

OTHER SAILORS
Leave us here to dream in comfort,
The ways of wisdom are hard.

UNICORN
Come with me to the heights of light,
Take me by the hand.

SOME SAILORS
We will come with you,
to the world of God.
We will not be enchained to the Devil.

OTHER SAILORS
Sweet is the devilry of this island.
We will follow the pleasant ways of the goblins.
In their chains we are safe.
Who knows if this unicorn can take us all.

UNICORN
Yours is the choice,
Your will is the way.

Your heart can ascend to the light
If you break the chains of the Devil.

(*One group stays behind, the other group goes with the unicorn. The unicorn and his following go forward. They are met by the Archangel Michael who holds out his hand to them.*)

UNICORN
There was a sleeper
Who became a dreamer;
He saw the sight
From depths to height
Of a spiral stair
Climbed by Angels fair.
They were ascending,
They were descending,
To Heaven they brought
Bright human thought,
On Earth they told
Heaven's wisdom of gold.
Now the Archangel's might
Brings today from the night
What that dream has foretold
In far ages of old.
He illumines with thought
All that Angels have brought,
Human hearts to inspire
With flames of Heaven's fire.

MICHAEL
Now the hour of bravery has come
Rise up to be rightly human.
Put down fear, put down desire,
Rise, to be crowned with Spirit's light.
Rise from the sleep of Earth
To live in the wisdom of Heaven.

UNICORN AND FOLLOWERS
We will climb the spiral stair,
We shall hear you calling there.

MICHAEL
He who on Earth overcame death

| | Has opened the ladder to Heaven.
Its guardian am I,
Who invites you to climb,
Who holds out my hand
To Christ-seeking souls. |
|---|---|
| UNICORN AND FOLLOWERS | We will follow your call,
We will climb to the heights. |

CINDERELLA IN EGYPT

The Persons and Divine Beings

AESOP
RHODOPIS, a slave
CHORUS OF MAIDENS (slaves)
MESSENGER
CHARAXOS, a Greek living in Alexandria
HORUS
FALCON OF HORUS
PHARAOH
CHORUS OF PHARAOH'S COMPANIONS

SCENE 1

A household in Greece with slaves under the care of Aesop.

AESOP	Come together, come to listen, slaves in name but clear in heart. Learn the wisdom from the gods given to souls of beasts and birds, hidden divinely in their nature. Beings of heart and soul abound, hidden away, but ever present, working in events that shape us, pushing, pulling at our fates.
RHODOPIS	Teller of tales, beloved master, much and often you have cheered us. Homeless, helpless, kept as slaves. Tell the tale to put out sadness.
CHORUS OF MAIDENS	Tell us what at heart you cherish, secret treasures of your mind.
AESOP	Listen to this. Helpful influences surround us sent by beings who wish us well; hindrances attacking threaten, sent by beings who wish us ill. What confusion, what collision, human doings still beset. How distressful, how perplexing are the muddled ways of men, pushed by some and pulled by others, hither, thither by these beings.
RHODOPIS	Do not the good prevail? Do not the gods protect?
AESOP	Wondering, the gods behold evil they may not forbid. Together evil and the good are stirred to one in human fate.

	And so compounded is our lot, partly joy and partly sorrow.
CHORUS OF MAIDENS	More sorrow has our fate than joy, harshness more than warmth of kindness. Are we by the gods forsaken?
AESOP	Beings with an evil purpose roam perversely through the world hearing whispered plans of people, snags inventing to frustrate them. Mischief spreading with design, they increase in skill and number. How shall good gods now proceed? How protect those of well doing, how to foster our endeavours that the good may grow and flourish?
RHODOPIS	Are the gods not also skilful, cherishing the good and right?
CHORUS OF MAIDENS	Shall the gods not beat and batter bad ones hindering our hopes?
AESOP	Cunning are the gods for they shelter in concealment those who work the grace of goodness, enriching the doings of people planned in good will and trust. Do you see them, find them, know them? Do you hear them, come and greet them? Mischievous are those you notice, dangerous doings you must fear. Devilry betrays itself. In the shadows are the good ones, working secretly their will, hidden behind the threats of evil, concealed through that which you most dread.
MESSENGER	Come, your doom is at hand, comfort and quiet are ended.

Cinderella in Egypt

	Say farewell to the teller of tales.
CHORUS OF MAIDENS	What is amiss, what threatens us?
MESSENGER	You are all called to the market. Old age besets your master. Quiet is what he most craves. He chooses companions for leisure, youngsters he sends away. Luck at the market be yours. You will bring wealth to this house.
CHORUS OF MAIDENS	Alas for us, our home is lost. Hard is our fate, bitter our woe.
AESOP	May the immortals protect you! May their divine grace shine upon you.

SCENE 2

A quayside in Egypt.

CHARAXOS, THE GREEK OF ALEXANDRIA	Well guided was I by the Fates, well-portioned am I in this land far from the place of my birth. Gardens and houses are mine, dwellings as pleaasant as those where my childhood was cheerfully passed. But alas, the passing of years has left me alone and disconsolate. Hades has swallowed the loved one whom I cherished with joy at my side.
	(*A trumpet sounds.*)
CHARAXOS	Ships come sailing from far-away lands. Who cares what they bring and provide? Old as I am, my heart is responsive, hope still lights up for what shall be.
	(*The chorus of maidens comes by led from the ship by Rhodopis.*)

CHORUS OF MAIDENS	Far over the sea, a great way off, sadly we journey against our will, sadly we wonder how it shall be when the bid is laid and the lot will fall.
RHODOPIS	Gracious the god who has brought us here over the sea to this lovely land. Hope shall be ours.
	(*Charaxos greets the slaves. The procession stops.*)
CHARAXOS	Mortals there are as gracious as immortal gods.
RHODOPIS	The smiling of your countenance reveals a gracious heart.
CHARAXOS	Speech like yours is from my homeland.
RHODOPIS	You are exiled, as we shall be. Is your lot good in this foreign place?
CHARAXOS	Richer by far is the wealth found in this place, wider the world of experience opened up in the land of Egypt. Travel on fearlessly with hope.
RHODOPIS	We are slaves set out for sale, threatened by buyers unknown, parted from all that we love, desolate, deserted and doomed.
CHARAXOS	Poor ones, you are wrongfully used. You are homeless and helpless. Come with me, if you will, to my home, dwell under my care. All shall have lodging and food. Wealth is mine, enough for you all. What price will the slave master ask? It shall be paid tonight to the full.
RHODOPIS	You will keep us together and protect us, slaves whom you cherish as children? How shall this be?

CHARAXOS	Desolate is my rich dwelling; laughter is not to be heard there. Teardrops are the sound of my fountains. Down to Persephone's realm, down to the shadows of Hades, descended the beloved of my heart. Wealth has its charms here above, but it is valueless below. The gods of Hades cherish my loved ones. Behold how I cherish these lost ones. Behold my petition by deeds upheld.
RHODOPIS	We will accompany you, good merchant.
CHORUS OF MAIDENS (*in procession*)	What is our fate, What have the gods ordained? Is this man's goodness arbiter of our lot? Are we to be rescued, Are we to be doomed?

(*The maidens go off with Charaxos.*)

SCENE 3

In the garden of Charaxos.

CHORUS OF MAIDENS	Hail to the gods on high! Hail to the helping ones! Sending us rescue at last. Pleasant are the ways of our master. Lovely the home he provides. May his heart be turned to us always. May his goodness forever endure.
CHARAXOS (*to Rhodopis*)	Borne here on the waves of fate, descended most surely from princes, royal in bearing in every gesture, you are a gift of the gods to myself. How can I call you daughter,

	though you reign in my heart forever?
RHODOPIS	Who were my father and my mother I cannot hope to discover. Nor do I need now for parents, having seen so devoted a father, found so loving a heart in yourself. Content would I be as your daughter, surrounded by maidens familiar So long was I dreading to lose them, fearing our fate and our parting. All of us have you embraced, all of us gathered around you. All of us homeless ones sheltered, lost children who now know a father.
CHARAXOS	My home was made ready with care, everything thoughtfully planned. Should the daughter descended to Hades Persephone-like rise again, she should for her welcome lack nothing. Not she appeared, but another, unknown but new-born to my love, deserving of everything lovely which in ignorance was here prepared.
RHODOPIS (*to the chorus*)	Come all of my maidens and friends, together we'll walk through the gardens admiring each flower in its kind, hearing the happiest bird song, attuned to the splashing of fountains.
CHORUS OF MAIDENS	Follow on, follow on in his footsteps, strange the land, stranger still is the host, giving hope of a home that endures, giving love where no duty commands.

(*The maidens play in the garden. Rhodopis emerges from a pool carrying her red slippers.*)

| RHODOPIS | Joy emerging from pain, hope out of fear, |

Cinderella in Egypt

new life out of slavery passed.
God whom we cherished and served,
prayers that are answered in him
seeking the child whom he lost,
finding the daughter unknown.
These are the gifts of the gods.
Hail to the Father Himself!

CHORUS OF MAIDENS
Hail to the gods who give answer to prayer!
Hail to the father who rescues the maidens!

(*The maidens play a dancing game, such as 'Here We Go Round the Mulberry Bush'. While they are dancing, the god Horus comes to look on.*)

HORUS (*contemplating*)
How do they pray to the gods,
mortals bound fast to the Earth?
Each passing joy is their wish,
each stab of pain is their fear.
Gods should give, should release,
bring joy and retrieve what is lost.
Gods should bestow what is asked,
their power should make them generous.
Immortal, be gracious to mortals.
What if the god gives more,
exceeding the prayers of the faithful?
Why merely give what is asked?
Why not send gifts in excess,
Where human hope is too simple and small.

Come my messenger, gather the prayer.
Come my falcon with the message of Horus.

(*The falcon appears, stopping to hear the command. The maidens bow down and hide their eyes.*)

FALCON	Speak to thy messenger, high god.
HORUS	From past to future my gaze extends. Charaxos shows the love bestowed by mortals. Powerful and greater is immortal love. Take one red slipper from her hand. Blest be the fate that follows.

(*The falcon takes the slipper.*)

HORUS (*to falcon*)	Be swift my messenger, away.

(*The maidens uncover their eyes. Rhodopis finds the slipper gone. She turns to Charaxos.*)

RHODOPIS	Alas, one of the slippers you gave me has been stolen.
CHARAXOS	How was it stolen? Who could seize it?
CHORUS OF MAIDENS	The god-like falcon swooped and it was gone.
CHARAXOS	Horus, the god, commands the falcon. What does this portend? What will has Horus? Happy is mortal life in harmony. We dwell together in this garden, sweetly would I live out my mortal days. Alas for us, a god immortal looks on our joy, alas, for me.
CHORUS OF MAIDENS	Gone is the messenger of the gods, flown away on the winds of Heaven. What he has gained, we have lost. Just the red slipper, just one of two. Fetch fast another, all is over then. Our happy mortal life begins again.
CHARAXOS	Shoe for the foot, foot for the ground. Will for the steps trodden on Earth.

Cinderella in Egypt

	Zest for the path by faith prescribed, joy in the future foretold in the sign. All this in the gift of the shoe. Alas, my hope and joy I gave away.
RHODOPIS	Thanks to you for bright hope, thanks for adventure to come, thanks for the shoes to travel on. Come with me, we go together. If there is joy, we laugh, if there is pain, we weep. Courage we have for the travelling, strength for the will of immortals.

(*All maidens join hands and dance.*)

SCENE 4

Pharaoh is in the courtyard at Amasis with companions.

PHARAOH	Let us confer on our troubles. Let us give thought to our scheme. Let thought for thought speak, let wisdom find words. Immortals will work their will, mortals shall follow on, inclining to hear, deeds of men shall fulfil intentions of gods.
CHORUS OF COMPANIONS	Great Pharaoh, we gratefully hear directions sent forth from your throne, knowing how closely you live with the gods Lending your ear to whispered wisdom breathed from the beak of the falcon divine, messenger of the immortals.
PHARAOH	He who sits on the throne must hear,

what he hears, he must speak.
But within he must listen often,
and hear the voice of his heart,
not the voice of a god, but a mortal,
not wisdom divine, but human.
Mysterious, distant are the voices,
heard both around and above us.
Hard they are to comprehend,
uncertain is their message.
How much clearer is the voice of thought,
how wisely formed are the concepts
that are grasped by the human mind,
but we are bound to the ways of the gods.

CHORUS OF COMPANIONS
Magnificent in wisdom are you!
Mighty Pharaoh, to whom we must turn.
Plants are we that would bloom in the Sun.
Splendid are you, with radiance divine.
We trust, we repose in your light.

PHARAOH
Companions quite other I crave,
awake to the powers of thought,
alive in the mortal mind.
What actions would then be prepared,
not directed by gods, but by ourselves?
Calling on powers like to theirs,
building a world that is human
where they, even they might dwell.

(*The great falcon of Horus swoops down and drops the slipper.*)

CHORUS OF COMPANIONS
What sign is now made by the gods?
Horus speaks with the falcon's voice.
We mortals are favoured by him.

(*Pharaoh receives the slipper dropped at his feet.*)

PHARAOH
Shoe at my feet but not for my foot.
Small it is, for a maiden to wear.

Cinderella in Egypt

What is the message, what shall I do?
Foot for the ground, foot walking on.
Earthbound foot sent by the bird.
Shall will be released by the gods?
Shall human will work on Earth?
Whence comes the shoe, from what foot?

CHORUS OF COMPANIONS
Search for the foot that sent the shoe.
Search where feet are small but strong.
Not among men but maidens afar
will be found that which brings new life.
What is the longed-for gift from Heaven?

PHARAOH
Search through the kingdom,
north and south. Go swiftly.
Such a sign shall not wait.

CHORUS OF COMPANIONS (*as they march away*)
To the south, to the north
from sunrise to sunset
down rivers, up mountains,
through cities, through deserts,
we travel, we struggle,
we carry the slipper,
the sign of our seeking,
man-made, but God-given.
What will it foretell?

(*Horus comes up behind them.*)

HORUS
Pharaoh calls for the power
wielded on Earth by immortals.
How dangerous a gift he seeks,
how far shall wisdom extend
to enliven the will of mortals?
But see how far the insight has gone
that instructed the will of this girl
who was sent by the wisdom of Aesop
to the greatness of will in Charaxos.
Were these men divine? They are mortals
who bear within them the gifts of gods.
May the foot for the slipper be found.

SCENE 5

In the garden of Charaxos, beside the fountain, the maidens are dancing as before.

CHARAXOS   How can a man of years be blessed
with such joy after long sorrow?
Loveliest of girls is Rhodopis,
daughter to me as beloved as she who
went down the dark path to Hades
before her loveliness was fully known.
What shall become of Rhodopis in time?
Is she not by right of rescue mine?
But is she not god-gifted in herself,
who should fulfil her promise for
herself?

(Rhodopis enters holding one red shoe.)

RHODOPIS   We who were slaves have a most loving
father.

CHARAXOS   You were slaves when I bought you. Now
I set you free. Your life is yours, your fate
is yours to find. My love shall go with
you, wherever that may be.

RHODOPIS   Upon my heart a shadow fell, cast by the
falcon as he seized the shoe. What shall
the portent bring?

(Pharaoh's chorus of companions enter.)

CHORUS OF   From the south to the north,
COMPANIONS   from sunrise to sunset
we travel, we struggle,
we suffer in vain.
Where is the fellow
for the slipper we carry?
We are weary with searching
while the Pharaoh awaits.

CHARAXOS   The Pharaoh awaits? For what do you

Cinderella in Egypt

	search? By whom are you sent?
CHORUS OF COMPANIONS	So simple a matter, so weary the search. A bird brought the slipper, just one. And the other, where is it? Where can it be?
RHODOPIS	My shoe was seized by the bird of Horus but whither was it taken? Do you bring it again?
CHORUS OF COMPANIONS	The slipper is here for the foot that it fits.

(*The two slippers are produced and they make a pair. Rhodopis puts them both on her feet.*)

CHORUS OF COMPANIONS	The weary way is ended. The long search is completed. We long for refreshment, for rest.
CHARAXOS	Here in my house you shall find both. Are you messengers from the Pharaoh? How can this be?
CHORUS OF COMPANIONS	The holy falcon, bird of Horus, flew with the slipper to Amasis. He dropped it at the feet of Pharaoh while he conversed with counsellors. The wonderful sign from a god must be answered, its meaning sought. The Pharaoh waits for her who wears the shoe. Come to Amasis.
RHODOPIS	A sign from Heaven must be followed. Father, must we part so soon?
CHARAXOS	Messengers care for you at command. You do not go alone to your fate. I will follow to share what befalls. The gods cannot forbid, nor Pharaoh refuse.

SCENE 6

Pharaoh's court at Amasis.

PHARAOH   What is the message of Horus?
                  What sign does he send by the bird?
                  One slipper, but feet there are two.
                  Who walks on one? Two feet touch the
                      Earth.
                  Two for walking, for running, for
                      dancing.
                  Who performs on Earth, but with two
                      feet, two hands?
                  Why did Isis seek long for Osiris?
                  What belongs to two that cannot be for
                      one?
                  What willing is born between two?
                  Shall the lost shoe reveal what is twofold?
                  Shall those that are coming bring the
                      other?

                  (*Enter the chorus of companions with
                  Rhodopis, and Charaxos following behind.*)

CHORUS OF   The sign is fulfilled, the search is done.
COMPANIONS   We bring mighty Pharaoh the shoe.
                  With the shoe the foot, with the foot the
                      maiden.
                  Hail to the shoe sent by the bird.
                  Hail to the maiden called by the shoe.
                  Hail to Horus, who made the fate.

PHARAOH   Maiden of the red shoes, Horus has sent
                  you.

RHODOPIS   Great Pharaoh, you called, I came.

PHARAOH   The shoes are not paired.
                  Two heads are joined with feet and hands.
                  You are sent to be my Queen.
                  Our thoughts shall interchange
                  until we act by common will.

Cinderella in Egypt

The gods have given to mortals
what until now was theirs,
to act by thought on Earth.
Our hearts unite, our feet shall walk
    together.

(*Rhodopis points to Charaxos.*)

RHODOPIS   Here is he, who gave the shoes to me.

PHARAOH   He, being mortal, acted for immortals.
The god-sent bird has given the holy sign.
Welcome to you, O stranger prophet.
You brought to Earth what Horus
    planned.
Strangers are you both, sent by the gods.
Be royal guests today and ever more.
Remain for life, she being my Queen,
You being counsellor long years ahead.

CHARAXOS   Should the gods allow, be it so.

RHODOPIS   Brought by the shoes, I follow the sign.
Alone I accomplish little, with you much.
May all the years reveal through us
what was intended here by gods.

CHORUS OF COMPANIONS   Hail to the God who sent the sign.
Hail to the bird who brought it down.
Hail to the teller of tales from afar,
Hail to the doer of deeds at hand.
Blessing from Horus and those who
    foresaw,
who followed the sign and found it true,
who accepted the task sent by the heavens
that humans should work with immortal
    gods.

(*A sacred dance is performed.*)

THE LAD IN THE GOATSKIN

Based on a Celtic story

The Persons and Spiritual Beings

THE LAD
A GIANT
A TWO-HEADED-GIANT
A THREE-HEADED GIANT
KING
QUEEN
PRINCESS
REDHEAD
DRAGON
SEVERAL LITTLE DEVILS
GREAT DEVIL

SCENE 1

At the edge of the forest.

THE LAD
The world is full of splendid clothes
from head to foot, from top to toes,
they hang upon the passersby,
the coats flung wide, the hats held high.
The trousers go with flip and flap,
the shoes hit ground with many a rap,
the scarves are flying in the wind,
the gloves already left behind.
The skirts go swinging in and out,
now up, now down and round about.
How often all these clothes go by
in colours gay to catch the eye.
But some are seen to sit indoors,
while others stand about on floors.
For rest they hang around on hooks
or find in drawers their quiet nooks.
But people come when they get dressed
and rouse them from their quiet rest.
My clothes, where are they? is the cry,
and out they come. But what say I?
For me was borrowed from the goat,
this skin to make my only coat.

(*To the children in the audience.*)

How many clothes have you?
Alas, poor me, how better dressed
are you than me. Why? Have you
   guessed?
My mother, left alone, was poor
and could not let me pass the door
for shame that I should go undressed
to school, or work, unlike the rest.
The goat grown old breathed life away.
His coat is mine. In his array
I seek my fortune far from home;

the forest path I take alone.

(*To the audience.*)

Shall I go to the forest alone?

(*In the forest animals go by, and the lad sings a song.*)

Fur or feather
against the weather,
all creatures are dressed
in their very best.
Only I
go naked by
till something is found
to wrap me around.

(*The lad gathers branches and makes a faggot. He continues to sing.*)

A faggot for the fire,
a fire for the hearth,
a hearth for the house,
a house for the folk.

(*Enter a giant, roaring.*)

GIANT (*shouting*)	Out of my way! Off my land! Down you go by my strong hand.
THE LAD (*hitting the giant*)	Ding-dong down! (*The giant falls down.*)
GIANT	Oh woe to my head! I shall soon be dead.
THE LAD	What prayers can you say?
GIANT	No prayers do I know, only woe, woe, woe, again and again and again.
THE LAD	What can you give me?
GIANT	Take my club for today.

	I am off and away.
THE LAD (*picking up the club*)	Too heavy for me alone. I need a lift home. Come faggot, get flying for me.
	(*He climbs on the faggot.*)
	My faggot can fly far up in the sky, until with a bump he comes down with a thump.
	(*The lad goes off. After a few moments he comes back.*)
THE LAD	Off to the woods again today to fetch a faggot of sticks away.
	(*Enter a giant with two heads.*)
TWO-HEADED GIANT	Out of my way, off my land, down you go by my strong hand!
THE LAD (*hitting him*)	Ding-dong down.
TWO-HEADED GIANT	Oh woe to my two heads! I shall soon be dead.
THE LAD	What prayers can you say?
TWO-HEADED GIANT	No prayers do I know, only woe, woe, woe, again and again and again.
THE LAD	What can you give me?
TWO-HEADED GIANT	Take my pipe and play till they dance away all the livelong day. I am off and away.
	(*The lad mounts the faggot.*)
THE LAD	My faggot can dance

canter and prance,
until with a bump
he comes down with a thump.

(*He goes off and shortly comes back.*)

Off to the woods again today
to fetch a faggot of sticks away.

(*Enter a giant with three heads.*)

THREE-HEADED GIANT	Out of the way! Off my land! Down you go by my strong hand!
THE LAD (*hitting him*)	Ding-dong down!
THREE-HEADED GIANT	Oh woe to my three heads! I shall soon be dead.
THE LAD	What prayers can you say?
THREE-HEADED GIANT	No prayers do I know, only woe, woe, woe, again and again and again.
THE LAD	What can you give me?
THREE-HEADED GIANT	Wound and burn do no harm with this charm. I am off and away.

(*The giant gives the lad a bottle of ointment. The lad then rides around singing.*)

THE LAD
My faggot can glide,
on gusts of wind ride,
until with a bump
he comes down with a thump.

(*Pause.*)

Enough of giants one, two, three.

The Lad in the Goatskin

What fortune has the world for me?

(*Pause.*)

The world is full of many woes.
The mind is boggled by the blows
that fall on people far and near
and now the strangest thing you'll hear.
Some careless people fall downstairs,
Others are taken unawares
by ladders, roofs and falling slates.
Some stub their toes,
some bang their pates,
some miss the bus,
the bus hits back,
some take wrong turns,
some miss the track.

(*To the children in the audience.*)
What about you? Are you in trouble too?

Some cannot sneeze,
some cannot stop,
some shed salt tears,
some not a drop,
some get too fat,
some pine away,
and all would have it the other way.
Now the King's daughter in dismay
has never laughed for many a day.
So dumb to laughter, deaf to cheer,
has she been now year after year.
What should become of her hereafter
if she remains bereft of laughter?

(*To the children in the audience.*)
Can you laugh? Then you are not like
  her.

What shall be done to set her right?
I intend to try with all my might.
Off I fly on the faggot my steed

to bring her help in her time of need.

SCENE 2

The courtyard of the King's palace. The King, Queen and Princess are watching tumbling tricks along with bystanders. The King and Queen laugh, but not the Princess.

KING	What tricks these merry folk can do. They make me laugh, but what of you?
QUEEN (*to Princess*)	I laughed but once. And you, my dear, are you in heart for better cheer?
PRINCESS	Alas, I could not when I would be moved to laughter as I should. For seven long years I try in vain while these good folk make merry game.

(*Enter a red-haired man.*)

REDHEAD	How patiently my sweet Princess you bear the pain of your distress. Almost you laughed, it seemed so near. Do not give up, but persevere.

(*Enter the lad with the club.*)

KING	Who is this stranger?
QUEEN	Why is he here?
REDHEAD	He heard the news proclaimed and came to stare.
THE LAD	From far away I heard it said the Princess had resolved to wed. As she is laughterless, she knows she shall the laughter-maker choose. Shall I be he? I face the test of how to make her smile at least.

(*To the children in the audience.*)

The Lad in the Goatskin

	What do you say? How can I do it?
REDHEAD	You fool in goatskin, nameless one, the test is not for you, begone!
	(*To the people around.*)
	Take him, push him, pull him outside!
KING	You go too fast and far.
QUEEN	Stop, there shall be no fighting here.

(*The lad holds up the giant's club and swings it over their heads. The groups of people begin to stagger about, to bump into each other and turn on each other.*)

THE LAD	The club swings, the knob rings with a thud on the head. In a row down you go, you shall fall one and all. No blood shed, no wound red. You turn and sway in dizzy play, you roll about in silly rout.

(*The Princess laughs aloud.*)

QUEEN	Do you hear? The wonder is done! Do you hear? The rescue has come.
KING	Who could help but laugh, they perform such silly stuff.
REDHEAD	Only a fool in goatskin he; it was mere chance.
KING	But he had a great success.

	At least he needs some proper dress.
THE LAD	One laugh has come, two more to be done.
KING	Come to be dressed in our very best.

(To the children in the audience.)
What shall he wear?

(The scenery of the courtyard can be kept for the next two scenes, i.e. until the end of the play.)

SCENE 3

THE LAD

The place is full of splendid clothes,
they showed them hanging up in rows.
The King called maids and men in haste
to show them off and ask my taste.
They brought out shirts with socks to match.
What colours gay there were to watch.
They offered every style of wear
in coats and cloaks with more to spare.
They measured arms, and legs and feet,
that suits should fit and shoes be neat.
How could I choose with such a choice,
I could not even find my voice.
A goatskin was my only dress
and now on every side they press
to fit on garments fair and fine,
to tell me they shall all be mine.

(To the children in the audience.)
What would you choose?

They brought a coat of golden thread
with hat and feathers for my head,
and shoes with buckles for my feet

The Lad in the Goatskin

	to clothe me when I would retreat from botheration about dress! They brought me back, to my distress, to deck me out in this array. They held me fast—I ran away.
REDHEAD	The King enquires with great dismay why you took off the fine array.
THE LAD	How can the Princess laugh once more? A double task is still in store, for me, who under such a stress moves better in his goatskin dress.
REDHEAD	A dragon roams across the land, destroying crops at every hand. He fills the people's hearts with fear, they dare not strike or come too near. The King is helpless in this plight, some strength of yours would come aright.
THE LAD	Where is he found? I shall not fear to seek him out and find him near. (*To the children in the audience.*) Shall I go to look for the dragon?
REDHEAD	He is not far beyond the hill. I make for home, I've had my fill. (*There is a distant sound of roaring.*)
THE LAD	My magic skill shall help me best. Now courage for another quest. (*The lad disappears. The music of his pipe is heard, mixed with roaring. He returns, leading the dragon, who dances about.*)
DRAGON	What a mishap, the silly chap makes me dance gets me to prance,

	stops my growl, chokes my howl with the sound of the round his pipe can play the livelong day.
LAD (*to the children*)	What shall I do with him? Shall I take him to the Princess? (*To the dragon.*) Along with me you shall dance away, to King and castle we take our way. You grumble and growl, but all in vain, you should keep your breath to dance again. (*Enter the King, Queen, Princess and entourage.*)
ALL (*shouting*)	The dragon! the monster! away, away!
THE LAD (*singing*)	A roundelay, the pipe will play till your feet keep the beat, till you swing in a ring, spinning round to the sound of the skirl in a whirl. (*All begin to dance at the pipe's music. The Princess laughs aloud.*)
PRINCESS	What whirling, what skirling, the dread of the dragon is done!
KING	She laughed again, I heard her laugher plain.
QUEEN	She laughed once, and laughed again.
PRINCESS	I laugh and cannot stop laughing.

The Lad in the Goatskin

REDHEAD
: Stop, stop the dance!
  I'll explain.
  The piping does it, I complain.
  Why must I dance and prance again?
  Let me complain.

(*They all have to dance on.*)

THE LAD
(*to the children*)
: Can you dance too?
  The giant's pipe will sing its song
  until the dragon does no wrong
  and follows to his mountain home
  where he belongs, no more to roam.
  The Princess laughed to see him prance,
  to see the folk in dizzy dance.
  The club made magic for her cure,
  the pipe was medicine for sure.
  Whenever merriment is due
  the pipe will surely have the clue.

REDHEAD
: I complain. You've danced yourselves silly.

(*The lad leads the dragon away.*)

SCENE 4

The lad has returned.

KING (*to the lad*)
: And is the dragon far away?
  Has he now other games to play?
  Is he content with country air?
  Will he forget our city fair?

THE LAD
: The dragon found a dragoness,
  I introduced them at a guess.
  His temper has become quite mild,
  so happily is he beguiled.
  Your fears are needless, for my part
  one burning wish consumes my heart.

>   The Princess who has laughed but twice
>   cannot be cured till she laugh thrice.
>   Please tell me how this may be done
>   that I her favour shall have won.
>
>   (*To the children in the audience.*)
>   What is to be done?

KING
>   It will not be my great delight
>   to have her laughing day and night.
>   A quiet life is what I prize.
>   My worries are so great a size
>   that merriment is out of place.
>   My enemies come on apace,
>   and, from a report I hear,
>   which may prove true I much must fear.

THE LAD
>   By token of her merry laughter
>   two-thirds I have won your daughter.
>   No concern can be so great
>   as that which shall decide my fate.

KING
>   The Queen it is who will not rest
>   until the Princess with the best
>   can laugh and laugh just as she will.
>   My royal plight is far worse still;
>   my soldiers like to stay at home,
>   my sailors do not want to roam.
>   My enemies are far more keen
>   on war than I have ever been.
>   Your help I need much more than she,
>   will you a great deed do for me?

REDHEAD
>   He cannot do it, just you see,
>   much better you rely on me.
>   I am the one to be the Prince,
>   and not at all this silly dunce.

KING
>   I doubt it, but you both can go
>   to find the magic for our woe.
>   A flail is hid in Hell deep down.
>   The Devil made it for his own.

The Lad in the Goatskin

Had we that flail, our foes would fear
with warlike threats to come so near.
In peace would every year pass by,
my Kingdom prosper happily.

THE LAD (*to the children in the audience*)
Shall I go?
How do I get to Hell at once?
The Devil shall regard the dunce.

KING
The Devil's always to be found.
Knock, and you find him underground.
He lets you in without delay
and then assumes that you will stay.

REDHEAD
First to see how he fares,
and not be taken unawares,
is far the best for me.

(*The lad knocks loudly. A great din is heard of howling, whistling and squeaking—like the music of Stockhausen. A group of little devils open the door.*)

LITTLE DEVILS (*together*)
Come in, come in,
don't fear the din,
we like it loud.
We're also proud
to embellish Hell
with many a smell,
with nasty smoke
to make you choke,
with fiery heat
to make you sweat,
with spike and dart
to make you smart,
with sting and weal
to make you squeal.

(*The Great Devil comes in and speaks pleasantly.*)

GREAT DEVIL
A guest is very welcome here.

	What can we do to give you cheer? How do you come to seek us out? You come for something here, no doubt.
THE LAD	You have a flail of magic strong. A loan of it to take along until my enemies have fled is what I wish, just as you said.
GREAT DEVIL	The Devil's magic I can lend but let me give you warning, friend, it brings the user and his foe an equal measure of its woe.
THE LAD	The risk is mine. Please bring the flail.

(*The lad covers his hand with the ointment. The devils, giggling, give it to him, expecting that it will burn him. He grasps it.*)

THE LAD (*to the Great Devil*)	This weapon surely will not fail. Thanks for your courtesy. Farewell, farewell.
GREAT DEVIL	You cannot go like that from Hell. The flail is hot that you should burn, the gate is shut, that you should turn. Against the rules you play the game. Come back at once for very shame.

(*The little devils all jump at the lad, but he beats them back with the flail which is too hot for them—they cry and hiss. He goes past them and knocks open the door.*)

THE LAD	Farewell to Hell.

(*The door bangs. Above, at the palace, the lad offers the flail to the King, Queen and Princess.*)

THE LAD	Here I come to bring the flail. The Devil howled without avail.

The Lad in the Goatskin

It puts your foes in such a plight
they surely will not want to fight.

(*Redhead tries to take the flail. He yells.*)

REDHEAD

It's hot as Hell!

(*The lad drops it and puts ointment on
Redhead's hand. Redhead yells again,
mixing relief with anger.*)

REDHEAD

What a relief! What a grief!
I hate this lad, he makes me mad.
The pain has gone, but he has won.

PRINCESS

What a botheration. What a sensation!
There's nothing for it but to laugh.

THE LAD
(*to the children in
the audience*)

Did you hear? Did she laugh for the third time?

(*He sings a song.*)

Hear her laugh, sweet Princess,
once, twice, thrice, and not less.
Has the spell now been ended?
Has the heart now been mended?
Are the tasks truly done?
Is the venture really won?

KING (*to Queen*)

Are you glad of the laughter
laughed by our daughter?

QUEEN (*to King*)

As glad as only you can be
who have this new security.

KING

The flail can injure friend and foe;
it must lie safe where none can know,
in danger only to be found. Put it away!

PRINCESS

He mended my weary heart,
he showed me laughter's art.
He learnt from the giants their spell,
he went bravely the Devil to quell.
What can I do but love this lad,

	just such a dunce in goatskin clad. His three brave deeds have surely shown that only he should share the throne.
QUEEN	If he puts on some proper clothes I can accept what you propose.
KING	If he is keeper of that flail your wish shall certainly prevail.
THE LAD (*singing*)	Sweet Princess, be my bride. Sit me down at your side. Let your heart tell me true I may love such as you. Do not scorn to love a lad though he come in goatskin clad. Did you hold him for a dunce? Make him now to be your Prince.
	(*The lad plays his pipe and they all dance away. Then he comes back dressed in good clothes.*)
THE LAD	They dressed me up in splendid clothes, they covered me from top to toes, they made me walk in shoes so tight, they gave me coats to fit aright. It never was so hard I know to move, to sit, to rise and go. What's more, the Queen has made decree that courtly manners learnt must be, that even this poor simple dunce must deal with pomp and circumstance. How hard to change as she requires, to satisfy the royal desires. I won the Princess three times over and now I have to win her mother. Love's labour shall not prove too hard, herself shall be my true reward.

WHAT TO DO WITH THE DRAGON

The Persons and Spiritual Beings

SEVERAL ANGELS
ARCHANGELS—
  MICHAEL
  GABRIEL
  URIEL
  RAPHAEL
THE DRAGON
SEVERAL DEMONS
PEOPLE—
  BAKER
  TAILOR
  CARPENTER
  GARDENER
  HOUSEWIFE
  NURSE

In Heaven a group of Angels.

ANGELS	What a bother what a bother, the stars are quaking, the heavens are shaking, our work is undone as soon as begun. Who brings the trouble, who makes the muddle?
ARCHANGEL	The Dragon brings trouble, he makes the muddle.
ANGELS	Stop him, stop him.
ARCHANGEL MICHAEL	Who will stop him, rampaging about with roar and with rout?
ANGELS	Great ones, lordly ones help us with speed.
	(*The Dragon comes by with demons making a noise.*)
DRAGON AND DEMONS	Rabadacabra, rabadacabra.
ANGELS	Ooh, he is getting bigger and bigger.
	(*Three Archangels in a group, Gabriel, Uriel, Raphael.*)
ARCHANGELS (*together*)	We heard you calling, we heard him roaring.
GABRIEL	My work is done through the power of the Moon bringing life to the Earth.
URIEL	My work is done when the thoughts of God are made known through the world.
RAPHAEL	My work is done

	when sickness is healed. The Dragon keeps out of my way.
ARCHANGELS (*together*)	We are working God's will each by dint of his skill. Being powerless to fight we are sharing your plight. Let Michael with the sword, the fighter of the Lord, contend with the foe who works us such woe.
	(*The Dragon and demons come back.*)
DEMONS (*to Angels*)	It's such fun, jostling the stars and shaking the constellations. Come and join us.
	(*The Angels run around stopping their ears.*)
AN ANGEL (*to demons*)	You are making mischief.
DEMONS	Hooray for mischief.
ANGELS	It must be fun to make mischief.
DEMON	Come with us, to be a demon, look here.
	(*He puts a demon's hat on the Angel's head and drags him away.*)
ANGEL	Stop, let me go back.
DRAGON	Rabadacabra.
	(*Michael appears with sword.*)
MICHAEL	The power of the Lord gives strength to my sword. The Dragon makes trouble getting Heaven in a muddle, the stars in disarray,

the planets in dismay,
the Angels losing heart,
the world falling apart.
This must stop.

(*He holds the sword over the Dragon who is frozen in position.*)

Sun's light enfold me,
Sun's warmth uphold me,
that courage quicken,
that courage ripen,
into strength for the deed
to be done in Heaven.

DRAGON Few words to say,
fighting is my way.
On with the fray.

(*He and the demons start to fight with Michael but they get mixed up with each other and fight themselves. Michael stands over them. Dragon and demons are frozen.*)

MICHAEL What shall be done with the Dragon? Can we slay him?

OTHERS Oh no.

MICHAEL Can we keep him?

OTHERS Oh no.

MICHAEL Can we bind him?

OTHERS Oh no.

MICHAEL Can we throw him out?

OTHERS Where shall he go?

MICHAEL Who will confront him, where shall he go?

OTHERS Send him below

MICHAEL	Down he shall go, down, down below.
OTHERS	Down, down below.
	(*He and the Angels throw the Dragon down.*)
DEMONS	Oh woe, oh woe.
DRAGON	Down we go to work our woe, down is as good as up for working woe.
	(*A group of people busy with jobs.*)
BAKER	Knead the dough and bake the bread.
TAILOR	Cut the stuff and sew the seams.
CARPENTER	Saw the wood, hammer the nails.
GARDENER	Dig the ground and sow the seed.
HOUSEWIFE	Clean the house and lay the table.
SCHOOLTEACHER	Call the children to come to school.
NURSE	Put them to bed and give them pills.
	(*They are happy and sing at their work: 'All things bright and beautiful'. Then they begin to be sad and start quarrelling.*)
BAKER	The bread does not rise.
TAILOR	There is no one to help me.
CARPENTER	You are getting in my way.
GARDENER	I'm much too tired.
HOUSEWIFE	You all make such a mess.
SCHOOLTEACHER	You don't do what I tell you.
NURSE	It's all gone wrong.

(The Dragon and demons come by.)

DRAGON	Rabadacabra ...
DEMONS	Ranting and roaring, hustling and bustling, troubling and muddling, wherever we're found, confusing, contorting, deranging, dispersing, exploding, upsetting, you find us around.
PEOPLE	What's this, what's this, a dreadful dragon. We don't want him.
BAKER	Where do you come from? Go away.
TAILOR	We want to be left alone.
CARPENTER	We got on well without you.
GARDENER	Why should we put up with you?
HOUSEWIFE	You will make a mess of everything.
SCHOOLTEACHER	You are in the wrong place. Who sent you?
NURSE	Stop all that noise.
DRAGON	Nowhere to come from but there, nowhere to stay but here.
DEMONS	Nowhere to stay but here.
DRAGON	Down we go to work our woe. Down is as good as up for working woe.
PEOPLE	What shall we do with the Dragon? He has nowhere better to go. The Angels threw him over. Who will help us now?

What to do with the Dragon

DEMONS	Oh, woe, oh, woe.
	(*The Archangel Michael appears.*)
MICHAEL	Sun's light enfold me. Sun's warmth uphold me, that courage quicken, that courage ripen, into strength for the deed to be done on Earth.
PEOPLE	What shall we do with him?
MICHAEL	Will you slay him?
PEOPLE	We cannot.
MICHAEL	Will you stop him?
PEOPLE	We cannot.
MICHAEL	Will you throw him out?
PEOPLE	We cannot.
MICHAEL	Confront him, confront him.
PEOPLE	How?
	(*Michael sings an old round with some new words, and the others join in.*)
	'Come follow, follow, follow, follow me. Call the Dragon, call the Dragon where he too may busy be.'
	(*The people set to work. Michael takes the Dragon to each person.*)
DRAGON	
(*to the baker*)	Let me heat the oven.
(*to the tailor*)	Sew with the machine.
(*to the carpenter*)	Change to power tools.
(*to the gardener*)	Discover the tractor.
(*to the housewife*)	Let the machine do the work.

(*to the schoolteacher*)	Have you heard of visual aids?
(*to the nurse*)	The same drug will do for everything.
DEMONS	Ranting and roaring, hustling and bustling, troubling and muddling, we want to be there, confusing, contorting, deranging, dispersing, exploding, upsetting, we're eager to help.
PEOPLE (*to Michael*)	Can we trust them?
MICHAEL	Sun's light enfold you, Sun's warmth uphold you, that courage quicken, that courage ripen into strength for the deeds to be done by people in whom God's goodness lives in abundance.
DRAGON	Rabacadabra . . .

(*Song sung all together: 'Come follow', etc.*)

THE OFFERING

The Persons and Spiritual Beings

CHORUS OF ANGELS (OR A SINGLE ONE) WITH FULL BASKET(S)
CHORUS OF ANGELS (OR A SINGLE ONE) WITH EMPTY BASKET(S)
CHORUS OF ANGELS (OR A SINGLE ONE) WITH HALF-FULL BASKET(S)
AN ARCHANGEL
TWO GOOD-FOR-NOTHINGS
LIGHT DEVIL
DARK DEVIL
DOLOROUS, a sorrowful man
A STRANGER
THREE PASSERS-BY
MERCIFUL

CHORUS OF ANGELS (OR A SINGLE ONE) WITH FULL BASKET(S)	Baskets filled up brims at their fullest, scents overflowing, tastes at their truest, blossoms full blown, fruits at their ripest, brought as the offering, the token of harvest.

Where ripened the fruit? Where blossomed the field? And where was the garden that such increase would yield?

My heart was the garden, my lifetime the ground, where the blossom of goodness, turned to fruit, will be found. |
| CHORUS OF ANGELS (OR A SINGLE ONE) WITH EMPTY BASKET(S) | Our baskets are empty, our blossoms were frosted, the buds shrank unopened, the fruit was all wasted. There is nothing to offer, no token of harvest, no savour of goodness to bring to the Highest. The heart's garden is sunless, its produce is blighted, with evil intentions, with wishes affrighted. No Angels can offer what is blighted by evil; rejected as dregs, it is good for the Devil. |
| ANGELS (OR ANGEL) WITH HALF-FILLED BASKET(S) | Our baskets show sadly, our provision is least, what can be offered does not look of the best. How shamed are we Angels, |

The Offering

but good actions shed light
and goodness is cherished
though the showing be slight.
What shall be done
with these remnants of good?
How sadly we Angels
bring all that we could.

ARCHANGEL What shall I offer at the throne of God?
What shall I declare to the Lordly Ones?
The star-dwellers look earthward,
they gaze down at the star-born below,
asking: we gave them of our substance of life,
we gave it graciously, but what do they give?
What ascends from Earth to Heaven,
what is the answer to Heaven from Earth?

(He looks into the baskets.)

ANGELS WITH FULL BASKETS Receive our offerings.

ANGELS WITH EMPTY BASKETS There is nothing, nothing here.

ANGELS WITH HALF-FULL BASKETS Only the human people can do good.
Angels must take what they can get.

(The Archangel gathers the baskets and goes away. Two good-for-nothings come by.)

1st GOOD-FOR-NOTHING What are we here for?

2nd GOOD-FOR-NOTHING I often wonder what to do with myself.

1st GOOD-FOR-NOTHING We are not like animals;
they always know what to do with themselves.

2nd GOOD-FOR-NOTHING	We exist, but what is it all about?

(The Angels with empty baskets begin to throw them away.)

ANGELS	No one brings goodness to fill full our baskets. No deeds of great meaning are done to ease suffering. We give up, we opt out, we carry the baskets but do nothing to fill them. The good deeds of people, the kindness of hearts inspiring their prayers, are the offerings we need. There is nothing to bring.

(Two devils appear.)

LIGHT DEVIL	Listen to me. You can be my servants, bustling and busy, never sad.
DARK DEVIL	Listen to me. You can be my servants, obeying my orders, never glad.

(The Angels with the empty baskets put on the clothing of demons.)

ANGELS *(chanting)*	Dreadful demons, soul-destroying, trouble-makers, peace-disturbers, good admiring, evil doing, inclined to Angels, doomed to demons, here we come to work our woe.

(They disappear.)

(A man called Dolorous comes into his room in great distress.)

The Offering

DOLOROUS	At last I came away alone. They had set on me from all sides. No one heeded what I had to say, or took account of my principles. There was no accusation. How could there be? My responsibilities were carried out without fail, but I am out all the same, discarded, rejected, of no standing. I am entirely alone now since she went off, complaining so often of the narrow life here, of the restrictions, of my constant attention to my job. It is loss all round and loneliness.
DARK DEVIL	Accept me as the Prince of this World. Take the power of Mammon at its value, for them and for me.
LIGHT DEVIL	Despise them, the mean spirited ones; ignore them, rise above their opposition.
DOLOROUS	I thought to be alone. Who are you?
DARK AND LIGHT DEVILS (*together*)	We are your life mates, at hand to put a word in at all times.
LIGHT DEVIL	You would do well to listen. I can lift your head high above the misery they provoke with their sordid judgements. Listen to me.
DARK DEVIL	You would do well to listen. My advice is to your advantage.

	You have tried to believe that the power of money is not everything, but it really is.
LIGHT DEVIL	Do not stay here so sadly. Escape with me.
DARK DEVIL	There is no escape. You are back where you started.
DOLOROUS	I will not listen. You do not help, you haunt. Oh, who will help me?
DARK DEVIL	You have not lost me. Come my way.
LIGHT DEVIL	You will not lose me. Come with me.

(*A stranger is passing by and he stops at the door.*)

STRANGER
He passed me in the street
and turned in here.
Such despair in his face,
such dread in his gait.
Shall I knock?

(*He goes up to the door and pauses.*)

It is not my business.
He is a passer-by.
Is his misery mine?
He might take it amiss
if I knock.
Why should I share his trouble?
What is he to me?
I do not like to interfere.

(*He walks up and down.*)

DOLOROUS
Haunting voices from my own heart.
To be alone is danger,
but whom can I importune?

The Offering

The nearest have all gone.

(*The stranger, who has walked away, comes back and knocks.*)

STRANGER — I went, but I am compelled to come back.

DOLOROUS (*within*) — Someone knocks. How can I face a stranger. It can only be a stranger.

(*Second knock.*)

DOLOROUS — No one would knock but a stranger.

(*Third knock.*)

STRANGER — If no one answers, I shall leave.

(*Dolorous opens the door. The devils go into the shadows.*)

DOLOROUS — Are you looking for me?

STRANGER — We were passers-by.
I saw a great need.
That is why I am here.

DOLOROUS — I am someone with a ruined life.
What shall I do?

STRANGER — If you are ruined in one place,
start in another.

DOLOROUS — I belong to this city of Jerusalem.

STRANGER — Break your ties. They are broken already.
This city is a place of such order,
there is no room to move
but out and on, to start again.

DOLOROUS — You do not know my story.
You do not realize, until I tell,
how I was rejected, how I failed.

STRANGER — I am not concerned with your past.
My concern is with your future.
You should let go of your misery

	and start a new life—move on.
DOLOROUS	Where? How?
STRANGER	Jerusalem has rejected you. Leave it behind. Call it a prison fenced in by laws and regulations. Walk out, walk on elsewhere. Do you remember Jericho? That is a place to be at liberty, to forget, to get rid of miseries.
DOLOROUS	I ought to work, to build my life again.
STRANGER	Not so soon. You are not wanted here, by no fault of yours, no doubt. You will be welcome in Jericho. All the more if you have money for lavish spending.
DOLOROUS	I am not without wealth. What I have shall go with me, since saving is useless now. You recommend Jericho?
STRANGER	So full of fascination. Do not hesitate. Take the road to Jericho.
DOLOROUS	You knocked. You shared my misery. You brought a sign of hope. You deserve more thanks than I can say.
STRANGER	Fare you well.
	(*They wave to each other and go off in opposite directions. Dolorous takes to the road, carrying a full basket.*)
DOLOROUS	I travel a lonely road, why did I not invite a companion? Since I am among the hills, I sense danger in the darkness. Is it good to be alone?

The Offering

(*He turns anxiously.*)

Have I really left my responsibilities?
It was my choice to take much on myself.
I wished to make life meaningful,
to work for success, to have what I deserve.
But I found failure.
If I am welcome in Jericho,
it will be for my store of money.
I wished to have the wherewithal
to make a true offering to the Angels.
But what have I now to offer?
I am just escaping.

LIGHT DEVIL Here is devil's work to do.
Here is a man on his own,
without a sense of direction.

DARK DEVIL Here is devil's work to do.
Here is a man too stupid
to find a sense of direction.

LIGHT DEVIL You turned to me
when you got above yourself,
escaping alone.

DARK DEVIL You called on me,
when you took your money
to make friends in Jericho.

(*The devils reappear with the two good-for-nothings, catching them from behind, whispering in their ears.*)

DEVILS (*together*) Do it, down him, work him woe,
take what is his, don't let him go.

GOOD-FOR-NOTHINGS (*together*) We're not doing anything.
We don't want to do anything.

(*The demons push the good-for-nothings, but they hold back.*)

GOOD-FOR-NOTHINGS	Leave us alone. We are idle. We want to be idle. Go away!
DEVILS	Work woe, we tell you, work woe.
GOOD-FOR-NOTHINGS	You are pushing and pushing. It is devil's work.

(*The good-for-nothings rush on Dolorous and knock him down, scattering his goods.*)

DOLOROUS	Stop, stop, you are thieving.
GOOD-FOR-NOTHINGS	Shut up. Might is right. We're miserable, so you shall be miserable too.

(*They run off.*)

DEVILS (*together*)	What we said, they have done. What misery is now begun! It's best to run.

(*They both run, leaving Dolorous lying hurt and helpless.*)

1st PASSER-BY	How dreadful. Who has done this? It shouldn't be allowed. It ought to be stopped. But what can I do? One person on his own? He cannot help himself. I'm very sorry for him. Of course, such wickedness should not happen.
LIGHT DEVIL	You could not have put it better. Keep out of it.

(*First passer-by goes off.*)

2nd PASSER-BY	What is this? It must be an act of robbers. He must have been overpowered.

The Offering

	What a shame! It's very wrong.
	What's to be done?
	Perhaps he did something to bring it on himself.
	He took risks or made a mistake.
	I will call the police; it is their job.
DARK DEVIL	You have done the right thing.
	Make someone else take the trouble.

(*Second passer-by goes off.*)

DOLOROUS: Please help me, help me to get up.
I am in such pain in all my limbs.

(*An Angel holding a basket of good deeds comes to look. He turns and beckons. A third passer-by comes in and is led by the Angel to Dolorous.*)

DOLOROUS (*groaning*): Help me to get up.
I am in such pain.

(*Merciful bends down and helps Dolorous to sit up.*)

MERCIFUL: How did this happen?
Were you set upon?
Who did such violence to you?

DOLOROUS: They came upon me from behind.
I was alone and could not fight them off.
There was more than one—at least two.

MERCIFUL: Have you been robbed?

DOLOROUS: Where is my basket?
It has disappeared.
Yes, I have been robbed.
All that I have is lost.

(*He sits with his head in his hands.*)

MERCIFUL: What have you lost?

DOLOROUS	There was so much that I strove for. To have the chance to work hard, to make something that could be of value, to have made a place in the world for myself, to stand for what I believe is right, all this I have lost. I have nothing, I am nothing. What I founded myself has been ruined by others. Failure, not brought about by me, is my lot. How can others so ruin one's life? All the fruits of my efforts are lost.

(*The good-for-nothings come past, throwing about the treasures from the basket.*)

GOOD-FOR-NOTHINGS	No use to us, worthless stuff, throw it out.
LIGHT DEVIL	Wastrels, you are good for nothing.
DARK DEVIL	Fools, you are good for nothing.

(*The Angels come and gather all up into their baskets.*)

ANGELS	We take what was your endeavour. You will see it no more, but it is not lost. It is your offering to be taken up to the throne, to be an offering of the Angels to the Highest. Offered for you, when you did not choose to offer.
ARCHANGEL	I offer up what was yours; it becomes one with the history of the world. It is a promise worthwhile for the future; it is your life-work offered up, not to yourself, but to the Divine.

The Offering

	Yours is the new life beginning now.
MERCIFUL	Take what the Earth gives for the healing of wounds.

(Merciful puts ointment on the wounds of Dolorous. The Archangel begins to throw shooting stars. The Angels try to catch the stars.)

ANGELS Gathering stars from the fields
where they ripen in the heavens,
we bring them to heal you.

(The devils fail to catch the stars.)

MERCIFUL It all depends on the new start.
Do not look at your ruined life,
at all that you have lost
by malicious interference.
Look for the open doors, the opportunities.
What you wished to achieve
might have become your limitation.
Now the horizon is far and open.
You are not bound by what you have done.
Now you can begin over again.
Unencumbered you walk on.

DOLOROUS My strength has gone.

(The Archangel throws shooting stars. The devils cannot catch them.)

DEVILS Reaching for stars,
we could use them well;
dissolving stars,
they escape from us.

ANGELS Reaching for stars
thrown down from Heaven,
gathering them up

from the Archangel's hand.

(*An Angel brings a star to Dolorous. He holds it in his hand. He begins to get stronger. He stands up by himself.*)

DOLOROUS: Where shall I go? Where do I begin?

MERCIFUL: Ask your own heart.
I will walk with you on the first part of the way.
All has disappeared that you meant to take with you.
All that you expected from your own efforts and aims has gone.
Others took the treasure of your life.
It was thrown away. But Angels gathered it. In Heaven it thrives for the future.
Seeds of spirit have been planted.
They will ripen and send their fruit
down into the field of Earth. For Man's nature it is to live here by what comes from above.
Your failure is a growing force for times to come. We make offerings without knowing that they were asked for, without intentions.
But there, where we are immortal among immortals, we shall know what is intended. Ask him (*pointing to the Archangel.*)

DOLOROUS: Have you given me strength from Heaven through the star held in my hands?
For this grace I give thanks.

ARCHANGEL: My treasure in Heaven is the might of iron,
courage-bearing, strength-giving, heart-warming.
From the falling stars it descends,

The Offering

setting off sparks overhead,
sending sparks into human blood.
Courage flares, deeds are dared.
Thought seeks will, will seeks thought.
My grace kindles courage for new hopes,
calling for ventures, for high aims,
calling for the makers of history
to bestir themselves.

DOLOROUS Will you be my guardian?

ARCHANGEL As the guardian of mankind,
wielding the iron sword of light,
so shall you know me.
The courageous shall live in my grace.
Do not look back, look forward.
By your aims you shall be known.

(Merciful walks ahead, Dolorous follows him. The demons rush to meet them, to stop them.)

LIGHT DEVIL He will end up among the pleasures of Jericho.

DARK DEVIL He will end up a dismal failure.

(The Archangel steps forward and restrains them.)

ARCHANGEL Go back, be gone.

(The good-for-nothings rush in.)

GOOD-FOR-NOTHINGS We are miserable; we will make you like us.
We are going back; we will take you along.
We will go down together.

(They pull Dolorous, but Merciful throws them off.)

MERCIFUL Let him be. Do not hinder the new

	beginning.
GOOD-FOR-NOTHINGS	What about us? He is a failure like us. Who is to be saved?
MERCIFUL	We will forgive you, for you cannot forgive yourselves. Forgiven, you will find a new beginning.
ANGELS	Who will give us offerings for our baskets?
STRANGER	I will offer my good intention, my will to help.
MERCIFUL AND DOLOROUS (*together*)	We will give you acts of forgiveness born of the grace that flows to Earth from Heaven.
DEVILS (*together*)	Are we always to be cast out on whom the doors of Heaven shut?
ARCHANGEL	In the changing history of the world there are always opportunities to find redemption, to raise the fallen. Those whom you tempted may yet redeem you.
STRANGER	My good intention was not enough. May I be forgiven, who counselled unwisely.
ARCHANGEL	In the sky the stars are shooting, from my hand the stars are falling, courage quickening. Hope reviving, will increasing, thoughts enlivening, catch and hold them, cherishing seeds of light in human keeping, planted where the hearts are warming, grown in hope until the blossoming flowers of light will turn to fruiting, harvest ripe for human offering.

The Offering

Angels, basket-bearers, searching
human souls for that beseeching
which will make a worthy offering
heavenward sent by heartfelt praying.

(*The Archangel leads the Angels, with full baskets, away in a procession.*)

THE BUTTERFLY

Entities, Creatures and Spiritual Beings

THE SUN
THE MOON
THE EARTH
ARCHANGELS—
  RAPHAEL
  MICHAEL
CLOUDS
EAST WIND
FLOWERS
CATERPILLAR, later a BUTTERFLY
CHILD

The Butterfly

The Sun, Moon and Earth move together in a simple form.

SUN
I am the Golden One, giving light,
sending warmth, pouring life,
filling the airy spaces
through the widths of the world.

MOON
I am the Silver One, taking light,
turning gold into silvery moonbeams,
charming the waters
into rising and falling.

EARTH
I am the Dark One, seeking light,
the cold one, craving warmth,
the lifeless one, asking life.
The waters will not rise,
the seeds will not grow,
the surge of spring is bound fast.

MOON
The night of my waxing
shall rouse up the waters,
shall awaken the seeds,
shall loose the surge of spring.

EARTH
Moon's light, Moon's might,
give increase of growth
to all creatures and things
born of my being.
Sun's warmth, Sun's light,
bestow life of soul
on all creatures and things
alive by your might.

SUN
He who sends golden light,
she who sheds silver beams
will unite with Earth's darkness
where form-giving forces
fashion in substance
the likeness of all things.

MOON
Root, drive downwards.
Stem, shoot upwards.

Leaf, expand outwards.
What was born into form
take on substance of flesh.
What was hidden unseen
emerge into sight.

SUN

Blossom born upward,
seed closed inward,
scent streaming outward,
what was born in the dark
grow up towards the light;
what was sown in the depths
return back to the heights.

EARTH

Thoughts become dreams,
dreams taking on flesh,
form turning to life.
What was pondered in thought
transforms into shape,
what was hidden within
turns to beauty without.

(*The Archangels Raphael and Michael appear together.*)

RAPHAEL

In the season of sprouting
when branches are budding,
when leaves are unfolding,
when seeds are burst open,
in the upsurge of spring,
Earth brings from within
the thoughts that she pondered
in the darkness of winter.
She brings to the sunlight
by the strength of the moonbeams
what she heard from the stars
at the night of the year.
She turns it to beauty
embodied in substance
that the Earth is adorned
with the glory of Heaven.

The Butterfly

MICHAEL
In the season of fading
when the branches are bared,
when the leaves flame and fade,
when seeds fall to the ground,
in the outsurge of autumn,
Earth turns again inward
from the glory of summer
and calls to the stars.
She calls and they answer,
resounding, revealing
in the music of the spheres
their divine inspiration.

RAPHAEL
In the turning of seasons
the Archangels bring
their gifts to mankind.
At the coming of spring
Raphael breathes blessing
in the flowing of warmth.
He brings healing to men,
healing, for matter is hard,
healing, for the Earth is dark,
healing, for the body is heavy,
healing, for the mind is asleep.

MICHAEL
At the coming of autumn
in the brightness of fading,
in the sharp tang of cold,
Michael is heard calling,
calling to wakefulness of mind,
calling to courage of heart,
calling to life in the Spirit,
calling to redemption.

MICHAEL
(*to Raphael*)
Take the strength of my courage,
weave it into your blessing,
add your warmth to my strength
that courage bring healing.

RAPHAEL
Let our fellowship weave

from springtime to autumn
from autumn to spring.

(*Sun, Moon and Earth move round each other.*)

RAPHAEL
When Earth, Sun and Moon
now stand to each other
in the position of Easter,
my working begins.
I, Archangel Raphael, speak
and am heard in parables.
See my parable and hear.

EARTH
Sun, Moon and Earth,
we make the spring together.
Send down the sunbeams,
scatter the raindrops,
call up the strong winds.
The time of growing has come
for all living creatures.

(*Clouds come by dropping rain.*)

CLOUDS
Clouds sail through the sky,
Clouds scurry on the wind,
Clouds scatter rain
on shoot and soil.

(*The East Wind comes boisterously by.*)

EAST WIND
Wind blows mightily,
Gale roars gustily,
buffets with airy blows.
Clear away clouds,
bow down branches,
cause shoots to cower.

SUN
Who rushes and roars
on this morning in spring,
making din and disturbance?
East Wind, is it you?

The Butterfly

EAST WIND Rushing and roaring
the East Wind blows by.

SUN Be quiet, I say.
By my power as king
in the wide heavens
I bid you begone.

(*The East Wind becomes mild and slinks away.*)

CLOUDS Renewing rain
will melt hard husks,
and weave the threads of life
through the Earth's dust.

SUN Heartening sunlight
follows renewing rain.
The loving warmth of Heaven
comforts the weary Earth.

MOON Strength from the moonbeams
make sturdy stem and leaf.

SUN Light from the sunbeams
touch with colour every flower.

EARTH Burst little seeds,
push down your roots,
send up your shoots,
put forth your buds,
show your secret to the Sun.

FLOWERS Down drive the roots,
up thrust the shoots,
the blossoms unfold.
Earthbound the root,
water-fed the shoot,
starborn the flower.
We lay in the darkness,
we were deadened in cold,
we rise in the light,
we are quickened to life.

Stars sent us to Earth,
Earth gives us to the Sun.
What was born from above
shines back from below.

MICHAEL
(*to Raphael*)

Nature renewing herself in spring,
is this the parable?

RAPHAEL

There is more to come.

(*A caterpillar begins to crawl among the flowers.*)

CATERPILLAR
(*to Earth*)

These flowers grow upwards
into the sunlight
and hold their heads
high above the ground.
They dance with the wind
and hear what he sings.
Why must I crawl below
in the shade of the leaves?
I want to grow into the light.

EARTH

You are too heavy,
you eat too much.

CATERPILLAR

I can run very fast.

EARTH

You are always on the move
seeking something for yourself,
nibbling here, nibbling there,
you take all you can get.
Flowers turn to the Sun
and worship his light;
they grow to be like him.

CATERPILLAR

I too would shine like the Sun.

EARTH

You are wrapped tight
in your fat little body.
Looking after yourself
you remain as you are.

CATERPILLAR

I do not want any longer

The Butterfly

                to remain as I am,
to care for myself,
to get bigger and fatter.
Above shines the Sun
giving light to the world.
I too will live in the light.

EARTH	Small plump creature, you have great thoughts and wishes. You will need to change very much.
CATERPILLAR	Tell me quickly how to change, that I may live in the light.
EARTH	There is a sure way but full of danger. You will fear your life is over, that you are dead and gone before you will have changed into a creature of the Sun.
CATERPILLAR	Tell me, I am ready to die.
EARTH	He who came from the Sun to help the creatures of Earth brought life out of death. Take courage, little grub, in death, you shall find life.
CATERPILLAR	What shall I do?
EARTH	Spin a shroud soft and white to wind round your body. Cover yourself quite from end to end in its folds.
CATERPILLAR	And then?
EARTH	Go to sleep in the shroud. Your body will shrink and fade, will dissolve into juice, losing its shape and form.
CATERPILLAR	What will become of me?

EARTH	Lie quiet and wait. Die without fear into nothing. When you are nothing an Angel will come to you. He will bring the pattern of what you shall become. He will press it hard against the shroud. Through the shroud it will touch the skin. Through the skin it will press into the juice. You will feel a new body begin to grow, a new body, tender and delicate. Then you will live again, a new life born from the old.
CATERPILLAR	I will die to live.

(*The caterpillar begins to spin the shroud and sleeps in it. Then Raphael comes and gives him coloured wings.*)

RAPHAEL	Receive the pattern, created from the light by the power of the Sun. Receive the wings woven in the air from the rainbow's colours. Rise on the wings that free you from the Earth, towards the heights of Heaven.

(*The newly formed butterfly begins to move about and flutter its wings. A child comes by.*)

CHILD	Oh, there is the first butterfly. The spring has come at last. Sun, Moon and Earth have been working together to bring on the spring. I know that they make the spring.

The Butterfly

	But Easter, who makes Easter that comes in the springtime? Do you know Flowers? Do you know Clouds? Do you know Wind?
RAPHAEL	Ask the butterfly.
BUTTERFLY	I dared to die and lose what once I was. I felt the self I was dissolve away. I found myself again born of the light.
RAPHAEL	From death he was newborn to spirit life.
CHILD	I heard his secret. Tell me what it means.
MICHAEL	From Heaven He came to Earth, the Lord of all the World. From the house of the Sun He came to dwell upon the Earth. Into the darkness of death He plunged and overcame its power. In the strength of the Spirit He soared to resurrected life.
RAPHAEL	Christ it is who gives us Easter, gives us life born out of death. He has set His sign before us in the changeling butterfly. So the spring is changed to Easter.

ELEMENTAL BEINGS

Spiritual Beings, Creatures and Entities

THE SUN
THE EARTH
STONES
GNOMES
PLANTS
UNDINES
SYLPHS
A BIRD
A BUTTERFLY
SALAMANDERS
ANIMALS
A CHILD

SUN	Midsummer is here. On the arch of the sky I wend my high way. The world's creatures rejoice in the strength of my light. They bring forth their beauty at the touch of my warmth.
EARTH	Midsummer is here. The bright Sun in his glory calls forth his creatures to appear in his sight. World Father is he, Earth Mother am I. We cherish our children through the seasons and years.
STONES	Out of midwinter midsummer is come. Remember midwinter before you go on.
SUN	Turned away from the Earth at midwinter was I, deep in talk with the stars as they wheel through the world. Much from them I gathered and stored deep in my heart; their light shines in mine, their strength streams in my warmth.
EARTH	Turned away from the world at midwinter was I, in deep contemplation and quiet I lived while the stars from above to my listening heart whispered the secrets of the summer to come.
STONES	What you at midwinter

	heard said from the stars
we stones always hear
as we lie on the ground.
EARTH	What I thought midwinter
at midsummer is shown.
All my creatures come forth
to your Father the Sun.
SUN	You creatures of Earth
formed by thoughts from the stars
have grown up by the might
of my life-giving beams.
At midsummer now
one another we greet,
World Father, Earth Mother
and their children together.
STONES	We lie quiet on the ground.
The ground is quiet below.
From Heaven we have our shape.
To Heaven we turn our gaze.
GNOMES	We are the gnomes,
the friends of the stones,
going up and down
under the ground
where the metals flow
in veins through the rocks.
World secrets we hear,
world secrets we know;
how wise are the gnomes
who listen below.
PLANTS	We are the seeds
sending down roots,
pushing up shoots,
growing leaf on the stem,
crowning stalk with the flower.
Holding fast to the earth,
striving up towards the Sun,

	we live and in living give praise to the world.
UNDINES	We flow with the water, we rise with the sap. We form in the flowing, we weave in the growing. All that the water as quickening gives we let flow through the stem and form in the leaves.
SYLPHS	We swirl in the air, we weave with the light, we waken the blossoms to fragrant unfolding. We give them their colours, we teach them their shapes, we surround them with joy in the time of their flowering.
BIRD	All that streams through the air within me I bear as I fly on my wings. What I learn from the world as I fly on the air in my song I declare.
SYLPH (*to bird*)	Creature of air, wait for me once. Let us share secrets, embracing for joy.
	(*They chase each other.*)
BUTTERFLY	Of sunshine my wings are woven. In sunlight I flutter from leaf to flower. To Father Sun I give myself gladly.

EARTH	Where are the great ones
who keep you in their care?
At the heart of the blossom
the seed must be quickened.
SALAMANDERS	From above we come
from the world fire itself
to bring life-giving warmth
to quicken on Earth
the holy secret
of the seed new formed,
of the little sheath
that safely enwraps
the germ of the future,
the promise of life to come.
SUN	The World Father himself
sends you his messengers
to bring to the Earth
the warmth from the world.

(*Salamanders go round and touch the plants.*)

SUN	Where are the creatures
endowed with movement
who hop, skip and jump?
ANIMALS	We are living and growing,
we are moving and breathing,
we are sensing and feeling
from end to end of the Earth.
We obey the order
by which we were created.
We follow the pattern
taught by our Mother Moon
to each of our kind.
EARTH	Now at midsummer
to you, World Father,
I bring all my creatures

	to be enfolded to be new quickened, with your light from Heaven.
SUN	What do your creatures give, Mother Earth, as an offering to Heaven?
EARTH	Much have my creatures received from Heaven to give them life. To you, World Father, their gifts shall be made that you may bring them to the spheres of Heaven.
STONES	One treasure we offer to the heavens who give it: the forces of form that have given us shape shall stream upward again.
PLANTS	Fragrance we have to give from each cup open wide to the Sun. Forces of life we have that upward stream as we grow and prolong their spiral way up to the light-filled heights.
ANIMALS	All we have sensed and felt: the pain and the pleasure of being, hunger and eating of food, exertion and quiet rest. What limb and senses perceive we bring to be offered here.
BIRD	My singing is my offering.
BUTTERFLY	The dust from my wings I will offer.
SUN	Your offerings shall stream from the depths to the heights.

| | But one creature fails,
one voice from your choir. |
|-------|----|
| CHILD | Midsummer is here.
The grass has grown high.
I run and I play
while the Sun sends light
to show me the way. |
| SUN | Midsummer is here.
All creatures are bringing
the gifts that they offer.
What will you give? |
| CHILD | I am only a child
who runs and plays.
I have nothing to give. |
| SUN | You live and you move
and you give without knowing.
What have you thought and done today? |
| CHILD | I ran away from my mother
when she called to stop me.
I pushed over my sister
when she wanted to follow me.
I threw stones at the ducks
when they swam away from me. |
| SUN | None of this can my sunbeams
bear up towards the light.
You have done black things
that drop down into darkness. |
| CHILD | I have picked some flowers
for our sick neighbour,
and half of the strawberries
I found on the hillside
I keep for my sister.
My mother will know
how sorry I am,
for when I come home |

Elemental Beings

	I shall give her a kiss.
SUN	My sunbeams will gather all that belongs to the light out of your heart and carry it upwards. What is good in human hearts is the midsummer gift Father Sun will take up to the Angels of Heaven.
EARTH	Now at midsummer to you, World Father, our gifts we bring that you carry to Heaven. What will you give us again in answer? We receive our life from the heights above.
STONES	Give us the strength of form that our might may not cease.
SUN	The strength of form shall flow to you from the heights.
PLANTS	Give us the colours of the light and the joy of your warmth.
SUN	The light from the heights shall give you colour. The warmth from the heights shall give you life.
ANIMALS	Give us the power of life that flows on the moving air.
SUN	The flowing air shall bring the power of life that moves in your limbs and quickens the sense for pleasure and pain.
SALAMANDERS	While the Sun sends down

	his power to the Earth we will weave in the warmth.
SYLPHS	While the Sun sends down his power on the Earth we will weave with the light.
UNDINES	While the Earth continues to nourish her creatures we will flow in the water.
GNOMES	While the Earth continues to nourish her creatures we will work in the ground.
CHILD	While the Sun shines down and the Earth upholds I will seek what is good.
SUN	Look up, dear child, when the night comes on. Bright stars you will see that shoot through the sky and fall down to the Earth. Bright sparks from the stars falling into your heart will quicken your courage to seek what is good and do what is right. From an Angel of God the gift is sent down into your heart from the falling stars.
EARTH	By your heavenly gifts, dear Sun, we shall live, and to you shall be given our thanks and our love. My creatures, look up to World Father, the Sun, and say your thanks.

CREATURES Midsummer is here.
TOGETHER   We look up to the heights
           giving our thanks
           and receiving again
           God's blessing of light.
           We live from the light.
           We bring forth in the light
           our strength and our beauty.
           Dear Father Sun,
           dear Mother Earth,
           we give praise with you
           to the Light of the World.

           (*Sing: 'All creatures of our God and King'.*)

THE FIERY FURNACE

The Persons

CHORUS
HERALD
NEBUCHADNEZZAR
THE THREE—
  SHADRACH
  MESHACH
  ABED-NEGO
CROWD OF PEOPLE

The Fiery Furnace

HERALD (*shouting*)	Ho, ho, ho, watch out! Watch the omens for what is to come.
CHORUS	Alas, alas, disturbance again. Just give us ease and quiet.
NEBUCHADNEZZAR	In the greatness of grandeur, in the presence of power, as ruler of regions, as King over kings, on the Earth I stand here. None mightier, none grander.

(*The herald blows a trumpet.*)

NEBUCHADNEZZAR	What next? Where's the battle? Where's the crown that's immortal? High gods among stars reign immortal and worshipped. Shall I climb to their heights? Shall I wait to be dead, then divine? Not so. As a god living here, a pharaoh transcending the human— this is not yet accomplished. I would be worshipped on Earth by nations and tribes all together. Will not the gods lean over the rim of the heavens on high? Shall they not lower the ladder, invite me to climb on the stars to dwell, though human, among them?
HERALD	Ho, ho, ho, hear and obey! I call with the voice of the King.
NEBUCHADNEZZAR	The trumpet makes known to all the voice of the King.

> Call with music when words are divided.
> Call to the gods among the stars.
> Many instruments sounding on Earth
> shall summon the gods of the skies.

(Notes are sounded on a lyre for each planet, and representing seven different instruments.)

NEBUCHADNEZZAR
> At these sounds, you men on Earth bowing to the ground shall worship,
> knowing your King to be a god.
> Should you deny him worship,
> flames of a fiery furnace
> in death shall devour you.

(Note B sounds.)

CHORUS
> Moon, note B: the horn. Gliding downwards, silver light.

(Note F sounds.)

CHORUS
> Venus, note F: the pipe. Pleasing sounds her invitation.

(Note D sounds.)

CHORUS
> Mercury, note D: the lyre. Coming, going, all is movement.

(Note A sounds.)

CHORUS
> The Sun, note A: the trumpet. Shining, giving, the world is brightened.

(Note C sounds.)

CHORUS
> Mars, note C: the trigon. Surging forward, falling backwards, all is action.

(Note E sounds.)

CHORUS	Jupiter, note E: the harp.
    Thinking, knowing, wisdom waxes.

(Note G sounds.)

CHORUS	Saturn, note G: the bagpipes.
    Recollecting, the past is gathered in.

HERALD AND CHORUS (*together*)	Music made among the stars
speaks a language to the Earth;
hearts can hear in unity.
Call out the warning!
Now appears the golden image
set by the city of Babylon.
Glory be to our King!
Abroad his name is heard.
Worship is offered him on Earth.
Gods in the starry heavens
hear our acclaim to the Sun,
gilding his golden counterpart,
image of Heaven on Earth.

(The herald blows his trumpet.)

HERALD	Ho, ho, ho, hear and obey.

(All the instrumental sounds are repeated.)

CHORUS	Bow down to worship the sacred image,
calling the god of the Sun to answer,
to touch his human image in our King.

CROWD (*in chorus*)	We bow low to the ground,
worshipping the golden image,
divine as the Sun.

God-like our King,
adored is our god.

CHORUS
Through all the lands it travels,
famous the trumpet's message.
Life and death are dispensed,
handed to mortals by God.
Golden is the image of him,
acting as a god on Earth.
Divine are his actions among us.
Bow down, worship, be afraid.

(*All the instrumental sounds are repeated.*)

HERALD
Who is without fear, who disobeys,
who worships another god, a greater?
Who knows that God from Heaven
speaks in the hearts of men,
needing no image, nor gold?

CHORUS
Few there are, they of Jehovah's faith.
Their God speaks with a voice from within.
Faithful will they be, and bold.
Here they come, three men of merit:
Shadrach, Mesbach and Abednego,
set up to rule in the King's stead.
Prayers they send to Yahveh.
Will he uphold their faith?

(*Angry voices are heard shouting and swearing against the three.*)

Hear how the royal heart in anger burns,
threatening the three with dire death

within the hell of fiery flames.
What shall they do?

(*All the instrumental sounds are repeated.*)

NEBUCHADNEZZAR Bring out the three before me.

(*Shadrach, Meshach and Abed-nego are brought before the king.*)

NEBUCHADNEZZAR Declare the truth: who do you worship,
gods of mine, the image of gold and me?

THE THREE No answer is required. The God we serve
He can most surely take us from your hands,
deliver us from fiery, fearsome flames.
Were this not so and should we perish,
still will we not and never worship
idols man-made of sacred gold.

CHORUS Alas, their fate is made.
Hold fast, brave men.
Your mantles, hats and tunics shelter you.
Fiery the furnace burns,
sevenfold in fury stoked.
Who can survive such fearful punishment?

(*The three are thrown to the flames.*)

THE THREE
(*chanting in chorus from Isaiah 43:12–13*)
You are my witnesses said the Lord.
I am God and henceforth I am He.
There is none who can deliver from My hands.

	I work, and who can hinder it?
CHORUS	Fierce flames of fire burn harshly. Boldly the heroes walk into their fiery death. Onward they walk, and cheerfully. Friendly the fearsome flames burn on, friendly, as though they could not kill.

(*Nebuchadnezzar comes to inspect the scene.*)

NEBUCHADNEZZAR	Come all of you to see and watch.
CHORUS	O King, we come.
NEBUCHADNEZZAR	Were not the three bound and thrown to the fire? What do you see? What do I see? Four men walk freely in the flames. Who is the fourth? His shining form, like to the Son of God, is shown to me.
CHORUS	Who is He but the Son of God walking beside His fearless ones across the fields of flame?
NEBUCHADNEZZAR	Come forth, O faithful three, true servants of the highest God, delivered by His Angel's hand.
CHORUS	Come forth, you men of God Shadrach, Meshach and Abed-nego. Fire has not marked your limbs, fire has not burnt your clothing. God sent His Angel to shelter you. You trusted in Him and were delivered.

NEBUCHADNEZZAR Blessed be the God of Shadrach,
Meshach and Abed-nego,
who risked their bodies to keep
their faith.
His dominion is an everlasting
dominion.
His kingdom endures from
generation to generation.
He does according to His will in
the hosts of Heaven
and among the inhabitants of the
Earth.
None can stay His hand or say:
what dost thou?
He is the Most High and lives for
ever.

JONAH

The Persons and Beings

GOD
JONAH
CAPTAIN OF SHIP
MARINERS
FISH
KING OF NINEVEH
PEOPLE OF NINEVEH

God is on His throne. On one side the people of Nineveh are making violent gestures; their heads are covered with dark hoods. Jonah is sitting in thought.

GOD   Behold the city of Nineveh, great and mighty.
What do I see passing before me,
rising up from its many people?
I see much wickedness in heart and deed.

(*To Jonah.*)
Jonah, arise, take action.
Go to Nineveh, that great city.
Cry out in reproach against it.

JONAH   Nineveh, that great city!
(*rising in fright*)   It is a horror to think of.
My life will be consumed,
my days end in its wrath.

(*He walks up and down.*)

What is to be done?
Can a man flee from the Lord?
Can he withstand His commands?
Shall I sail away from here?
Nineveh is a hopeless place for me.

(*He approaches a ship's captain.*)

Where are you bound?

CAPTAIN   We set sail for Tarshish.
Where are you for?

JONAH   Tarshish is the place for me.
What is the fare?

CAPTAIN   Ten pounds will be enough.
Have you that much?

JONAH   Here is the money. Let me come aboard at once.
How shall the Lord follow me now?

CAPTAIN	What is that you say?
JONAH	I must flee away fast. The Lord will take away my life.
CAPTAIN	Can you hope to flee from Him? Come aboard if you will. Away we go.

(*On ship, stormy winds blow. Jonah sleeps.*)

GOD	Blowing and blasting, howling and hurling, ranting and raging, let the gales blow, fiercely and far. Let the storm howl. Let the winds rage. Let my bolts strike.
MARINERS	God help us! The Lord save us! The God of our fathers shield us! God Himself shall hear us.
CAPTAIN	Lighten the ship, throw over the cargo. Let the sea consume it that the people shall not perish.

(*The mariners throw out the wares.*)

Here goes, here goes.
Not things, but people.
Not possessions, but life.

CAPTAIN (*to Jonah*)	What of you, sleeper? Wake up, call on the Lord! He will hear your voice. Call, lest we perish.
MARINERS	Some evil genius is here. A wrongdoer is among us. Let us cast lots to find him.

(They hand round little sticks. The lot falls on Jonah.)

MARINERS
(to Jonah)
Who are you? Who brings such evil?
How did you cause it?
What is your work?
Whence do you come?
What is your country?
Where do you belong?

JONAH
I am a Hebrew.
I fear the God of Heaven
who made the sea and dry land.

MARINERS
What is this that you have done?
How can you flee from the Lord?
Can you hinder His will?
Tell us what we can do
that the sea quieten for us.

JONAH
Take me up, throw me into the sea.
The waves will cease. The guilt is mine.

MARINERS
Row, row against the wind,
row harder through the storm.

(The storm winds rage further.)

MARINERS
We beseech Thee, O Lord.
We will not perish for this man.
Save us from all guilt,
for Thou has done Thy will.

(They throw Jonah into the sea. The storm ceases.)

MARINERS
Receive, O Lord, our prayer.
We offer to Thee obedience.
We vow to Thee our faith,
and acknowledge Thy glory.

(A great fish comes by.)

FISH
Give God the glory.

	What has to be done now?
	(*The fish swallows Jonah.*)

JONAH
(*in the fish*)
	Three days, three nights
	I have dwelt in this fish.
	It has been my house and my temple.
	I called to the Lord in my distress.
	He answered my prayer.
	From the depths of Hell I cried,
	Thou didst hear my voice.
	Thou didst cast me into the deep,
	into the heart of the seas,
	till the flood was round about me.
	All Thy waves and Thy billows
	passed over me. Then I said,
	I am cast out from Thy presence.
	How shall I look again upon Thy holy
	   Temple?
	The waters closed in over me.
	The deep was round about me,
	weeds were wrapped about my head,
	yet Thou didst bring up my life from the
	   pit.
	O Lord, my God,
	when my soul fainted within me
	I remembered Thee
	and my prayer came to Thee.
	Deliverance belongs to the Lord.

GOD (*to the fish*)	Bring out Jonah. Spew him onto the land.
FISH	Give God the glory. Deliver me from such as he.
GOD (*to Jonah*)	Arise, go to Nineveh. Proclaim in that great city my message to its people.
JONAH	I could not flee from the Lord. Hidden in the fish's belly

	I found wisdom. God's word shall be in my mouth.
	(Jonah walks to Nineveh.)
JONAH *(chanting)*	Praise the Lord, O my soul, and all that is within me praise His holy Name.
	(At Nineveh, Jonah cries out three times.)
JONAH	Forty days and Nineveh shall be overthrown.
PEOPLE OF NINEVEH	Alas, the Lord reproaches us. Let us change our ways and repent.
KING OF NINEVEH	Let us all repent, let each one turn from evil, and regret the violence that is in his hands. Let us sit in mourning, each man with his beast. Let each be aware of evil desires, putting them away.
GOD	See Nineveh, the great city, how all its people turn from their evil ways, to walk in righteousness with the Lord.
PEOPLE OF NINEVEH	O Lord God, save us. We leave evil and seek good. Let us not perish.
GOD	The evil which should come on you shall be prevented. You shall not perish at my hand. Reject evil and cultivate the good. Hear the Lord and revere Him.
PEOPLE OF NINEVEH	Praise the Lord, O my soul, and all that is within me

JONAH (*to God*) Thou gavest me, O Lord, Thy word to speak
a message of dread, a warning to be feared.
Thou madest me a prophet of doom.

But Thou hast shown Thyself
a God of mercy, gracious, slow to anger,
repenting the threat of doom,
abounding in steadfast love.

I am put to shame before the people
to whom I prophesied much woe.
Take my life away, I beseech Thee.

GOD Do you well to be angry?

JONAH I do well to be angry, angry enough to die.

GOD Should I not have compassion
for Nineveh, that great city?
Should I not shelter its people,
a hundred and twenty thousand,
not knowing their right hand from their left,
with many good cattle?

THE ANGEL, THE DEVIL AND TOBIAS

The Persons and Spiritual Beings

ARCHANGEL RAPHAEL
TOBIAS
SARA
TOBIT, Tobias' father
DEMON
MAID
BIG FISH, represented by Eurythmy; words spoken off
RAGUEL, Sara's father
EDNA, Sara's mother

SCENE 1

In Heaven. Enter the Archangel leading Tobias and Sara, veiled, who then stand back to back, looking in opposite directions.

RAPHAEL
(*to Tobias*)

Look ahead!

TOBIAS

Down there?

RAPHAEL

Look towards the things to come.

TOBIAS

The woman sits waiting
sadly, but flashes of joy
gleam at the thought of the child.
A man stands erect,
conscious of duties ordained
by the holy laws of God,
but heavy in heart with grief.
The towers of a city rear
behind them, threatening.
Their fathers never toiled
to build those frowning walls.
That is not their home.
Will it be mine?

RAPHAEL

It is not their home.
They are your parents;
their hope is towards their child.
You go to a homeless people
where each himself must keep
alone his faith with God.
Go forth, young soul,
in strength of courage.
Take to Earth
the Spirit's power of healing.

TOBIAS
(*half turning to the figure of Sara*)

Must I go alone?

RAPHAEL

Go alone, but seek for her

on Earth, and you shall find.

TOBIAS Do you stay behind?

RAPHAEL You will forget me
and I shall find you.

TOBIAS I shall forget?
(*turning to Raphael
and speaking with
wonder*)

RAPHAEL The Lord bless you
and keep your ways on Earth.

(*Raphael pushes Tobias away from him.
Tobias walks reluctantly, then his step
quickens and he is away.*)

SARA The far-off voices are sad.
The clouds between them and us
are dark and fearful.
Let me stay behind.

RAPHAEL See how they long for you
who have no other child.
Your parents are awaiting you anxiously.

SARA A shadow looms over the house.

RAPHAEL The light you take shall be bright.

SARA Something fearful awaits me.

RAPHAEL A trial for testing;
a sickness for healing;
an evil for vanquishing.

SARA (*retreating*) No, it is too fearful.

RAPHAEL He who helps is there already.
In the hour of need
I will bring him myself.

SARA Do not force me to go.

RAPHAEL	The Lord Himself be with you and protect you in all things. Go forth, dear soul, to Earth, And heal your fear.

(*He leads her on; she goes reluctantly, turning back, and then hiding her face.*)

RAPHAEL (*alone*)	Behold in me a servant of Him enthroned in the world-heights of Heaven. Among the Archangels known, I wield within my rank a part of the might of God. My heart is a single flame lit by the fire divine, the world-heart of God Himself. Compassion has kindled the flame; compassion has given it life; and compassion I offer up to serve the Son in His task, to rescue the souls of men from the pains of sickness and sin. Poor souls, they struggle in grief until they can utter a prayer so fraught with the force of truth that it finds God's listening ear.

(*On Earth. Enter Tobit. He is blind and feels his way.*)

RAPHAEL	Here comes Tobit, an upright man who has fallen on evil days, having himself no blame.
TOBIT	Who is there? Where is Tobias? My sight dims day by day and makes me helpless before my time.

(*Raphael helps him to a seat.*)

TOBIT	Thank you, my friend

	for help to a stranger. I am waiting for my son; he will guide me home.
RAPHAEL	A home and a good son are comfort in time of trouble.
TOBIT	Home? I used the word wrongly. Our home is far from here, that land my son has never seen whence my people were expelled. Great wrong was done to us then and continues to this day; but the blame was partly ours.
RAPHAEL	How so?
TOBIT	My people lost their faith; so many turned away from worship of our God and left the prayers unsaid, the Temple was almost empty. I went myself to Jerusalem at the proper seasons but few went with me.
RAPHAEL	How could that be?
TOBIT	To keep the eyes fixed on a distant aim which later generations will achieve, they found it too remote.
RAPHAEL	Have their hearts no eyes?
TOBIT (*sitting up at the sound of footsteps*)	I thank you for your help. My son is coming. (*Raphael withdraws. Tobias enters.*)
TOBIAS	I have been looking for you, father, a long while now. You have passed the turning of our street.

TOBIT	I feared so, for today my eyes are dimmer than before. Blindness is creeping on me. It is the last misfortune of many.
TOBIAS	We must find a medicine.
TOBIT	I went in search of one today. The sickness is known, but not the cure. Give me your arm, and let us go; I must now rely on you, my son.

(*They go slowly, pausing now and then.*)

TOBIAS	I have always trusted you, father, to guide me on the path of life. In your actions you have kept faith with the principles you taught.
TOBIT	But so an upright man should do.
TOBIAS	I have seen very few so.
TOBIT	Early in life, still half a child was I, when first I saw the Temple of our fathers' God. There, in that hour, much was revealed as truth that early I had learnt as law and custom to obey. My inner eyes were opened to behold Him as true God, and Man as His creation, made in His image. I vowed a vow of youth to keep the image unspoilt and clear within myself.
TOBIAS	And that was in the Temple? At Jerusalem?

(*He helps Tobit to sit.*)

TOBIT	You have seen temples here in Nineveh,

　　　　　　　　　　splendid and huge.
　　　　　　　　　　That should be: God Himself
　　　　　　　　　　is great enough. But in Jerusalem
　　　　　　　　　　the Temple is small, so hidden away
　　　　　　　　　　you would not find it by yourself.
　　　　　　　　　　It is rich in treasure. But the wonder
　　　　　　　　　　comes when you stand within
　　　　　　　　　　and feel yourself in every part
　　　　　　　　　　answer what is around you.
　　　　　　　　　　What is man, that he be consecrated
　　　　　　　　　　to bear God's image in himself?
　　　　　　　　　　This thought lives in those walls.
　　　　　　　　　　Here are the temples made for mighty
　　　　　　　　　　　　gods;
　　　　　　　　　　but there, man knows himself in God.
　　　　　　　　　　I have known Man in that Temple.

TOBIAS　　　　　　Was this the vision that gave you faith,
　　　　　　　　　　in dangers and in homelessness,
　　　　　　　　　　throughout the years?

TOBIT　　　　　　　It gave me strength in homelessness.
　　　　　　　　　　But now my heart is faint
　　　　　　　　　　because of helplessness.

TOBIAS　　　　　　There goes my mother,
　　　　　　　　　　burdened with a load too much for her.
　　　　　　　　　　Wait, father, here at the corner;
　　　　　　　　　　I will help her home.

　　　　　　　　　　(*He runs off. Tobit tries to follow, but
　　　　　　　　　　bumps into the wall, then gets too far from it
　　　　　　　　　　and cannot find his direction.*)

TOBIT　　　　　　　My eyes! My eyes!
　　　　　　　　　　Their light has faded.
　　　　　　　　　　The world is dark and I am lost
　　　　　　　　　　without direction. Tobias, come back!

　　　　　　　　　　(*There is no answer. Tobias has gone.*)

　　　　　　　　　　Why should he come back?

His mother needs him the more
since I am useless.
They will both learn in time,
how much I shall depend on them.

(*He leans against the wall.*)

How have I deserved blindness?
I have obeyed the laws of God,
and kept the principles of an upright man
in prosperity and in poverty.

(*Raphael appears behind him.*)

RAPHAEL	Is suffering sent only by desert?
TOBIT	Who spoke then? I heard no footstep. Is that the voice of my own heart?
RAPHAEL	What can suffering achieve when it prepares for what is to come?
TOBIT	When it prepares for what is to come? No, suffering is prepared itself by sin.
RAPHAEL	Will not suffering bear fruit in time to come?
TOBIT	No, suffering must be the fruit of sin. My sin is greater than I knew or know. Or is it the sin of my people, laid upon me? The weight of sin is greater than I can bear.

(*Raphael walks around him and stands in front of him with arms outstretched towards him.*)

TOBIT   O God of our Fathers, Lord,
in truth Thy works shall endure,
in justice shalt Thou judge,
and in mercy Thy works perform.
Remember me. Look on my sin

and on the guilt my fathers gave,
and send me now release.
Before Thee we have sinned
and disobeyed Thy law,
until Thy hand reproved
with exile all our race.
The burden of my sin
lies heavy on my soul.
The guilt for others borne
oppresses me with grief.
Deal justly with me now
and set my spirit free
from this poor body's house.
Turn not Thy face away,
but take me to Thyself,
to Thine eternal spheres.
On Earth my life is void:
call me to life with Thee.

(*Raphael gathers up the prayer and takes it away. Tobias comes and takes Tobit by the arm.*)

TOBIAS   Come, father, we wait for you at home.

SCENE 2

Sara is sitting quietly with a book in her hand, but she is not reading. A demon enters and begins to circle round her.

DEMON   Mine, lady, mine
                you are and shall be.
                Mine to suck life from,
                mine to feel through,
                mine to act in your will.

SARA   The Lord save and protect me!
(*starting up and*   Oh that I be delivered from this
crying out)   tormentor.

(There is a clattering sound outside as her maid comes in with a vessel of water. The demon disappears.)

MAID
What is wrong now?
You have been quiet all day
after the last disaster.
Now you are crying out again.

(She puts down the vessel of water.)

SARA
Oh help me! Where shall I find help?
God Himself has turned from me.

MAID
Whoever was so helped as you?
No father nor mother
could be more patient and kind.
And have I not cared for you,
nursed you when you were sick,
sat by you in your dark moods
of fearfulness and tears?

SARA
You were kind, all of you,
but so helpless, so much at a loss.
The young men were not saved,
nor I released.

MAID
It was all done for the best: God knows
how many doctors were consulted,
and other clever people.
They said, again and again,
a husband would be the cure.
And you, being an only child,
your parents were doubly eager.

SARA
But it was all no use.

MAID
Worse than useless.
None of us have any satisfaction.
A good servant must have
a good mistress, who does well
her part in life, a wise wife

	and the mother of fine children. But it has been tried so often and failed. Where are the fine young men?
SARA	Is it not more than enough to be so cursed as I without reproach being heaped upon misery?
MAID	It is true. You are under a curse that touches all who come near. Only God Himself can release you.
SARA	We have prayed to Him continually.
MAID	Your mother prays long and often. You would think her worn to death. If the Lord has not helped you it is not because He has not heard what is expected of Him. As for me, I can only pray quickly, say what I mean, and be done. If the Lord hears me at all he doesn't get any explanations. It's my belief we're dealing with a devil that has got hold of you, and we are not going the right way about it.
SARA	Don't say so. Don't call on him. He will come back again. I have no strength to resist him!

(*The demon comes from behind and rolls the jug away from the maid. He laughs.*)

MAID	What's that? Who's there? What's happened now? Oh help!

(*She runs off to rescue the jug, which is heard clattering outside.*)

SARA
(*covering her face*)

She has truly said
that a devil takes hold of me.
My life is blighted and useless.
How can an evil spirit seize me
And use me for his ends?
Why did he destroy the young men and
    not me?
If only he would destroy me too!

(*Raphael appears in the background, unseen by Sara.*)

SARA
(*more quietly*)

But what of my father?
Old and full of sorrow, he would die
if I, his only child, were his reproach.
My life is in the hands of God;
it shall not belong to the Devil.

(*She kneels down.*)

Lord God, Thy holy Name
in all Thy works is blest.
My heart is turned to Thee
begging release from life.
Thou knowest the evil curse
that now is my reproach.
Thou seest my heart kept pure,
my name kept free from stain
without avail. My days are void
and purposeless. Why should I live?
My father's only child
gives him no joy nor hope.
Take me unto Thyself,
into Thy mercy's fold.
If this be not Thy will
have pity on my grief
and ease my useless pain
with purpose and with hope.

(*Raphael receives the prayer and carries it away. Sara withdraws. Enter Tobit, groping his way.*)

TOBIT
He should be back again by now,
but I cannot hear footsteps.
It may well take a long while
to find a man who knows
how to travel from here to Rages.
Tobias must fetch the money
I left there once in trust.
He will need it after I'm gone.
What's that? Tobias, is that you?

(*He reaches out his hands in the wrong direction.*)

TOBIAS
Here I am, father.
Such good fortune! I have found a man;
he knows the road and accepts our wages.
He is ready to be off at once.

TOBIT
What is his name? And his race?

TOBIAS
He is of our race and knows of you
from Ananias, his relative and yours.

TOBIT
Why, that is better than I hoped.
You should start as soon as may be.

TOBIAS
My mother makes the preparations
while I have come in search of you.

TOBIT
The sooner gone, the sooner back again.
My son, throughout our life
we walk in the midst of death.
Now death is very near to me.
To you I entrust your mother.
Care for her, as she cared for you.
Be mindful always
to dedicate your mind to God,
for He has given you life.
Give to your neighbour
what help you have to give.
Choose carefully your wife:

>   cherish her and your children well
>   in love and prudence through the years.
>   Trust those who serve you,
>   justly paying them their due.
>   Keep watch upon yourself
>   lest pride excite you overmuch
>   or fear cramp you to meanness.
>   Open your mind to other thoughts
>   than those you think yourself.
>   Above all else, bless God
>   and pray to Him for clear direction
>   of your way through life.

TOBIAS Dear father, your good words
have well described the life
that I have watched you lead
through all my growing years.
In uprightness of principle
I saw you walk, leading the way
along the road of life.
Now I must go my ways alone
and find myself in the world
homeless and fatherless, myself
and nothing but myself.
I shall remember how I knew in you
the picture of an upright man.

(Raphael appears, clad for a journey.)

TOBIAS Father, here is the man who goes with me.

TOBIT Friend, do you know the dangers
and conditions of the country?
Will you help my son in need?
He goes into the world alone,
and for the first time.

RAPHAEL We both go with God, in His care and blessing,
who is also with you.

	Have no fear, your son shall return.
TOBIT	I give him into your keeping, for the good of us all. Go with God.
TOBIAS	Come home, father, and comfort my mother. And the Angel of God watch over you both.

(*Tobias and Tobit go out.*)

RAPHAEL	In my hands I carried up their prayers to the throne of God. A greater strength than my own streamed from Himself to me, and from me shall stream to them. But the power divine must unite with the force of a human heart. The human heart must take hold of what nature enchanted keeps, that healing be rightfully wrought. This young man is untried; he should prove himself to himself.

(*Tobias returns, ready for the journey.*)

TOBIAS	Are you prepared to start at once?
RAPHAEL	I waited only for you.
TOBIAS	My father urges us to start, my mother fears to see us go. I am their only child to help them now in trouble. It's hard to say, in truth, if I should go or stay.
RAPHAEL	Do they not require the money left in Rages?
TOBIAS	Most certainly they do. My mother fears to lose her son

	more than she hopes to gain, however.
RAPHAEL	What does your own heart say?
TOBIAS	It thrills to the adventure. My duty to my parents kept me close till now. I know the world so little and myself am quite untried in all its ways. How should I learn without experience?
RAPHAEL	Your parents need from you that which you cannot give unless you find yourself. The You, you are not yet; it shall be fashioned from that which meets you from without, calling to life what dreams within. To stay behind from fear will gain you nothing. God sends His Angel to your aid and theirs. Let us go on.
TOBIAS	Lead the way. I'm coming with you.

SCENE 3

Sara is asleep. The demon is prowling round her.

DEMON	Mine, lady, mine you are and shall be. Not mine when you sleep and your soul has soared upward, not mine when you waken with clear mind turned outward, but mine when you dream, half asleep, through the daytime; mine to seize hold on.

(Sara turns in her sleep, as if dreaming. The demon comes nearer.)

DEMON
Waken, my lady,
but waken to dream out your days
giving service to me.

(Raphael appears and stands beside Sara.)

RAPHAEL
Your prayer was heard on high
and he who brings your helper
is far upon the road
leading him to this place.
An Angel is his guide
who shall with strength divine
confront the demon's might.
Waken today with hope
and put your fears away.

(The demon slinks away. Raphael stands beside her until she wakes.)

SARA
Was it a dream?
And was the message true?
So many times in dread
I woke from sleep.
Shall I dare to hope today?

(Sara gets up and walks away. The big fish appears.)

BIG FISH
Waters whirling, currents curling,
river running, fishes flitting,
weeds a-waving, gleams a-glinting,
banks a-basking, fish a-feeding.

Tumult-troubled stream is seething,
waves are writhing, fishes fleeing,
monster moving, all-consuming,
dealing death on every side.

Dreaded monster, who shall curb me?
Who withstand my power of darkness?

(Fish disappears.)

SCENE 4

Raphael and Tobias are on their journey together.

TOBIAS	We are far away from home and greeted everywhere as strangers.
RAPHAEL	Each day's journey is an adventure; the good traveller is he who returns different from what he was at setting out.
TOBIAS	I was born in exile and never knew my father's home. I was never quite alone without kith or kin till now. We are both homeless.
RAPHAEL	The secret of going forward is not to look backward. The secret of becoming one's self is to lose what is not one's self.
TOBIAS	Do my parents not need their son?
RAPHAEL	Not only *they* need help. Others will call upon your strength if strength you have to give. Recall the purpose you beheld before you passed the gate of birth. As yet you have not faced the test nor won the means to help.
TOBIAS	How shall that be?
RAPHAEL	Trees on a river bank make the most pleasant shelter. Let us rest awhile.

TOBIAS	I am hot and dusty, though you look cool and clean. I will go and bathe.
RAPHAEL	Go. I will wait for you.
	(*Tobias goes to the river; his voice is heard singing.*)
TOBIAS (*singing*)	Little waves lapping, cooling streams laving, deep waters enfolding while the river flows on. I float on the water, I swim in the current, I dive in the deeps, while the water flows on.
RAPHAEL	Beware! Look around!
BIG FISH	Who shall withstand me? I come from the darkness, from the hidden depths beneath the waters.
TOBIAS	Help! Help me away!
RAPHAEL	Turn back to face him.
TOBIAS	Help! Save me from danger!
RAPHAEL	Turn back! Take the monster. My strength shall be with you.
BIG FISH	Who shall withstand the force of the darkness, the darkness beneath you, the darkness within you, the dark shadow of death?
RAPHAEL	Seize him! Take him! Hold him fast!
TOBIAS	God, help me! Send an Angel! Help me now!

RAPHAEL	God Himself is with you. The Angel is beside you. Fight on to the finish.
BIG FISH	Away from the light, down to the darkness, dragged by my might.
TOBIAS	No, no! Light shall triumph!

(*Tobias drags the monster up towards the bank.*)

BIG FISH	Let me go, let me free! Light I endure not; to darkness I plunge.
RAPHAEL	Hold fast. He is wearied. The struggle is over.
TOBIAS	The Light shall prevail!
BIG FISH	Drowned in light my darkness dies. Fed on air my soul expires.

(*Raphael helps Tobias drag the fish's dead body on to the bank. Tobias sinks down.*)

RAPHAEL	The Lord has strengthened you, the Angel watched over you, and you have prevailed against the creature of darkness.
TOBIAS	All the while that I struggled I was in deadly fear.
RAPHAEL	But you fought on.
TOBIAS	I fought on in despair, not knowing how or why.
RAPHAEL	You were tested and found strong. Now you are required for a great task.

	You will have need of the fish.
TOBIAS	But why? For what purpose?
RAPHAEL	Cut the fish open. Yes, like that. Take out the heart, liver and gall. Put them away safely; you will need them.
TOBIAS	But, my brother, tell me, what use are the heart, the liver and the gall of the fish?
RAPHAEL	They are useful for healing. The heart and the liver can be burnt. The smoke clears away the fumes which demons make in sick souls when they hope to obsess them. The gall is a salve for the eyes. I will teach you how to use what you have won for yourself. You will soon need its magic.
TOBIAS	So, you made me attempt the struggle because you knew what would be needed.
RAPHAEL	I could not foresee the outcome. It depended on your courage, and your strength to prevail.
TOBIAS	Then neither could have done without the other. We have a long journey before us, and other tasks to do. Let us go.
RAPHAEL (*sitting quietly*)	Before long, on the road to Rages, we shall visit your kinsman Raguel.
	(*Tobias stops moving about, and looks surprised.*)
TOBIAS	He with a daughter called Sara? I have heard of her before.
RAPHAEL	You shall see her soon at his dwelling.

	She is fair in looks and wise in heart.
TOBIAS	I have heard a strange tale that seven husbands she had, and each had died at once. What if she cast her fancy on me?
RAPHAEL	By the destiny you had at birth, you more than any other have the right to her as wife.
TOBIAS	But she is beside herself, the prey of an evil demon.
RAPHAEL	She is bound to you already by the divine plan of destiny, and by the will of the children who will be born to you.
TOBIAS	Is she truly sent to me by the hidden will that guides the ways of my life? If she is, I can love her now. But she is possessed, unfit to be a wife.
RAPHAEL	She is tender of soul and pure in spirit. But she cannot protect herself from the threat of the demon who haunts her. Others must help and protect her. It is you who are sent to her rescue, and I who am sent to your aid.
TOBIAS	Together we should heal her. But how shall this be done?
RAPHAEL	You carry the medicine with you in that which you took from the fish. Burn the heart and the liver until the smoke rises and spreads.
TOBIAS	Do you mean it is my task to drive away the demon

	and rescue this troubled girl?
RAPHAEL	You are chosen and destined for this.
TOBIAS	It is a solemn thought indeed that I am needed for this task. Glad I am that you are with me.
RAPHAEL	I will go with you and we will both go with God.
TOBIAS	It is evening, but we should start at once. We could go a long way in the dusk before we need to sleep.
RAPHAEL	I am ready. Let us go.

(*They move off.*)

SCENE 5

Sara is walking. The demon comes and circles round her.

DEMON	Mine, lady, mine you are and shall be. Mine to suck life from, mine to feel through, mine to act in your will.
SARA	O Lord God, hear my cry, deliver me at last.
DEMON (*crouching*)	Cease your wailing and your calling; that Name I cannot hear. Your pure heart you may offer to Heaven. Leave me the earthly and baser part— and be quiet.

SARA
(*with more confidence*)
: The Lord shall deliver me out of your hands.

(*The demon shrieks and runs away. Sara turns to see Raphael standing behind her.*)

RAPHAEL: Your prayer is answered already.

(*Raphael stands back and calls Tobias to come forward. Sara and Tobias look at each other.*)

TOBIAS: I see you for the first time
and have known you always.
Who are you?

SARA: Are you he who is sent to help me?

TOBIAS: If you are she of whom I heard,
whose need for help is great,
who is called Sara—
then, I am he.

SARA: My name is Sara—
and myself am cursed
to bring great harm
to those who come too near.

TOBIAS: I am called Tobias.
This is my faithful friend
who came with me from Nineveh.

SARA: You have travelled very far;
you should refresh yourselves with us.
Here is my father's house.

RAPHAEL (*taking Tobias forward*): We will be the guests of Raguel.
Come in.

SARA (*to Tobias*): Consider before you go in.
There is still time for you to hurry on
as if you had not seen me.

TOBIAS: I have seen you already,

and my heart has recognized you.
It is decided.

(*Tobias takes Sara's hand.*)

We will put our trust in Him
on whom you called.
I pray that He may send us strength
and, at the last, true love
from heart to heart.

(*Raguel and Edna come to meet them. They greet one another.*)

RAGUEL (*to Edna*) How like he is to my relation, Tobit!

(*to the others*)
Good friends, from where have you come?

TOBIAS We come from those exiled to Nineveh.

RAGUEL Is Tobit known to you?

TOBIAS AND RAPHAEL We know him well.

RAGUEL Is he in good health?

TOBIAS He lives still in good health.
He is my father.

(*Raguel embraces him.*)

RAGUEL Come in at once and be refreshed.
How much you have to tell me of my friends.

(*They go away. The maid comes by carrying a big basket.*)

MAID Dear me! What commotion!
What stir in the kitchen!
What greeting of guests
after months of depression.
A handsome young man—

more so than the others!
Now what will happen?

(*She hurries off. The demon then comes by, prowling to the door.*)

DEMON

Will she escape me?
Curses in plenty
I put on the bridegrooms.
This one is different;
he has a companion
not of his race.
I smell out an Angel.

(*He looks in at the door and comes back.*)

The will of a man,
spirit devoted,
can it protect her?
What of the Angel
who walks close beside him?

(*The demon shrinks away. The maid enters again.*)

MAID

What commotion, dear me!
What preparing and cooking,
what serving and dining!
What talking and telling of news!
Now the matter is broached
which I first had suspected.
The youth seeks a bride; the girl wants a groom.
But they sent me away to fetch wine.

(*She hurries off. Raphael comes out of the house with Raguel.*)

RAPHAEL

By the rule of old custom
you should give him your daughter.
By the hand of the Holy One
they now are brought together.

The Angel, the Devil and Tobias

RAGUEL   That is true; but think what happened before.

RAPHAEL   Her true destiny it was
to be kept for Tobias.

(Tobias comes in with Sara, and speaks to the two.)

TOBIAS   Is it now settled between you?
We came to this place seeking Sara,
and before night it must be decided.
How otherwise can we help her?

RAGUEL   Then take her, for she is yours
by right custom, and the will of God.
He Himself save you from the risk
that is taken with your life,
and send you and her in all things
His mercy and blessing.
Give me your hands.

(Edna comes in and stands on one side; Raphael stands on the other.)

RAGUEL *(to Tobias)*   Take Sara to be your wife, my son,
according to custom and to the will of God,
who Himself brought you together.

(Edna kisses Sara, who weeps.)

EDNA   The Lord bless and keep you,
and bring you joy out of sorrow.

RAGUEL   Bless the Lord, O my soul,
and all that is within me
bless His Holy Name.

TOBIAS *(to Raphael)*   Will you give me your blessing and help?

RAPHAEL   The Lord Himself will bless and keep you.

TOBIAS (*taking Sara's* *hand again*)	The Angel of God will watch over us that, beginning in sorrow, we may live our days in joy.
RAGUEL	It remains to write the documents and seal them. Come into the house.

(*They all go in except Raphael. He fetches a brazier with burning charcoal. The demon creeps round watching. Raphael stands waiting to one side. The maid comes in again carrying sheets. The demon withdraws. Edna meets her.*)

EDNA	We should prepare the room for them now.
MAID	Seven times done before, now done yet once again. And the queer smell is here that always came before. Phew! It smells of death!
EDNA	Smell? What kind of smell? Is it in the room?
MAID	It's the Devil's own smell that he brings with him. Poor dear young man. So handsome!
EDNA	Stop stirring up fear. God may yet be good to us. I will help you spread the sheets, then we will go and pray.

(*They disappear through a door at the side which leads to the bedroom. The demon comes in and starts prowling towards the door, giving Raphael a wide berth.*)

DEMON	She is mine by my desire, she is mine by my will to enthrall human beings.

RAPHAEL	The Lord is my shield and my salvation, a very present help in trouble.
	(*The demon runs back as Tobias and Sara come out of the door from the bedroom. Sara is weeping.*)
SARA	In that room it happened. I cannot go in there again. How often have I wept and prayed, but to what purpose?
TOBIAS	Take comfort. You are mine and have been kept from others for me. He promised me that before we ever arrived. Look, he is keeping watch now and has set a brazier ready.
	(*He points to Raphael.*)
	Now, I wonder—yes, I understand.
	(*Tobias puts his arm around Sara.*)
TOBIAS	In my arms you shall sleep your sorrow away. Take courage. There is a remedy, if need be.
	(*They move towards the door. The demon rushes between them and the door, trying to pull them apart.*)
DEMON	She is mine by desire, she is mine by power of my deadly wrath to strike people down.
	(*Sara shudders and sinks down.*)
TOBIAS	Protect us, O Lord, from the evil one and shelter Thy children.
	(*Tobias takes the heart and liver of the fish,*

throws them on to the brazier. The demon is hit by the smoke and at first behaves as if he were drunk and reels round the stage. Raphael comes out and stands between him and Tobias. When the demon sees him, he shrieks and flies off. Raphael pursues him.)

RAPHAEL   Back, I banish you at last,
to where you belong by right!
The might of God shall bind you fast
in the realm of your race.

(*Raphael and the demon disappear.*)

SARA (*looking up*)   Is he gone, and are we free?

TOBIAS   He is fled; and we should pray.

(*They kneel down together.*)

TOBIAS   O Lord our God,
blest be Thy Holy Name.
The heavens shall bless Thee,
and Thy creatures here on Earth.
Adam Thou madest and Eve
to be his wife, in love united.
What was asunder
Thou hast joined together;
so may we two be now made one
in token of the hope
which Thou hast given to men on Earth.

SARA   Guide Thou our ways, O Lord,
Through all the years.

(*They both rise.*)

TOBIAS (*to Sara*)   Come in, dear love, in peace.
Sorrow is past and joy shall follow after.

(*They go through the door into the bedroom. After a moment Raguel comes from one side with a spade and the maid approaches from the other.*)

The Angel, the Devil and Tobias

RAGUEL: What are you here for?

MAID: It is so still and quiet.
A quite different smell is in the air.
Never was it like this before.

(*They both listen.*)

RAGUEL (*beginning to dig*): He was the most fitting husband
that could have been found.
But there is a curse on the poor girl.

MAID: You dig alone in the dark.
Are you making a grave?

RAGUEL: If he is dead, we'll bury him quietly,
no one will know—he was a stranger here.

MAID: Don't be so sure that he is gone.
He may live to take your daughter
away to Nineveh, as his wife.
There is no sense of disaster this time.

(*Raguel goes on digging.*)

RAGUEL: It is better to be prepared for everything.

(*The maid goes round the door of the bedroom and tries to peep in. She returns.*)

MAID: It is all peaceful there, with
a sound like breathing.

RAGUEL: It would be better to be sure.

MAID: Go in then, and look.

RAGUEL: That would be most unfitting—
but not for you perhaps.
Yes, you shall open the door
and see what has happened.

(*He rests on the spade and waits. The maid goes and returns quickly.*)

MAID: Praise the Lord and His Name.

	He is alive, and they both are sleeping. New born shall they be to joy after the frightfulness of the night.
RAGUEL	To Thee, O Lord, we give praise, joining in chorus with the Angels, with all good men of the elect, and with all creatures of the Earth. Thou hast saved our two children from the danger that came by night and given us joy in the morning. Keep them in mercy all their days.

(*He gives the spade to the maid.*)

	Fill up the hole with haste. I must go to her mother.
MAID	It would have been better to have made sure first.

(*Raphael comes in as the maid is filling in the hole. He looks on. She sees him and stops.*)

MAID	Praise be to God, this is not needed. A miracle has happened.
RAPHAEL	Angels of God go up and down among men, but they are not known for what they are. God sent you help.
MAID	But why are the troubles sent first? She was lovely in heart and form till the curse came on her.
RAPHAEL	Devils are at work in the world, not Angels only. The power of evil lurks.
MAID	But why should such harm be done, why so much suffered?
RAPHAEL	It is necessary that evils be overcome

	that sickness be rightly healed,
	that evil be transmuted at last.
MAID	That is a riddle beyond me.
RAPHAEL	Where would Asmodeus, the demon, be without the girl Sara?
	He had lost his place in the world;
	he interfered in human behaviour.
	But Sara kept her uprightness.
	The healing virtue hidden in the fish
	could be released at last.
	The one whose life is joined to hers
	was sent when the time was right.
	The Angel of God has guided them
	in all their ways in answer to their prayer.
	The demon is released from doing harm;
	the girl is grown from innocence to wisdom;
	and the man has proved himself to himself.
MAID	But look what we went through!
RAPHAEL	How else could so much be achieved?

(*Tobias comes out.*)

TOBIAS (*to Raphael*)	My friend, it is through you,
	the stranger from the street,
	that all our fear is turned to joy.
	She is healed and life begins.
	What next should we undertake?

(*He notices the maid and the spade.*)

	What is afoot here?
MAID (*hastily*)	Sara will be calling you now you are awake.
RAPHAEL	Give thanks to God always
	and bless His Holy name.
	Come with me to Raguel,

and I will then unfold the plan
for obtaining the money
held in trust for your father.

(*Raphael and Tobias go off.*)

SCENE 6

Tobit enters, sits down and listens.

TOBIT	Listening, listening, for days I have been listening for his footsteps.

(*Tobias and Raphael enter.*)

RAPHAEL (*to Tobias*)	Go to your father quickly; rub the fish's gall into his eyes.
TOBIT	Whose is that voice? Tobias, are you here again?
TOBIAS	Be of good hope, my father.

(*He embraces him, rubbing the gall into his eyes.*)

TOBIT	My son, my son! What is this pain? My eyes, my eyes!
TOBIAS	Look up, father, look up, and see!
TOBIT	Blessed be Thy Name, Lord God. Blessed be Thy holy Angels. Thou hast taken pity to heal me. My son is come, and I see him.

(*They embrace.*)

TOBIAS	Dear father, we are safely home again, and I have brought to you a daughter, Sara, my wife. She is outside waiting for you to welcome her.

(They go to the door and Tobias brings Sara in.)

TOBIT
Welcome, daughter.
God bless you and your parents.

SARA
The Lord be with you, father,
and keep our ways together.

TOBIAS
Does my mother wait in the house?

TOBIT
She thinks hourly of your coming.
But we must not forget your companion
and how well he has cared for you.

TOBIAS
It is not enough if we offer
half of what I have brought.
See what he has done for us.

TOBIT
It is his due.

RAPHAEL
Hear first what I shall tell you.
Give praise and thanks to God
for the mercies He has shown;
exalt His holy Name
for the answer He gave to your prayers.
Walk in your ways in righteousness
that the power of your prayer increase.
Give good to those in need
for God's mercy given to you.
Remember that they who sin
destroy themselves their life.
I take farewell of you now
and, departing, reveal to you
who I am, and for what I came.
When, despairing, you prayed to God,
when Sara prayed in her grief,
I gathered your prayers in my hands
and carried them up to Him.
The Holy One sent me Himself
to bring healing for your pain.
I am Raphael, one of the Seven

	who present the prayers of the saints. I go from the twilight of Earth to stand in His holy Light.
TOBIT	Forgive us that we did not know you.
TOBIAS	Nothing that I have done could I have done alone. But that an Angel went with me I never knew.
RAPHAEL	By the will of God I was sent; to Him your praise is due. One of His chosen servants has walked on the road of life some little way with you. God be with you in times to come. I go up to Him that sent me.
TOBIT	Praise the Lord, O my soul, and all that is within me praise His holy Name.
SARA	You gave us health and hope of life. We shall offer thanks through all our days in head, in heart and in hand.
TOBIAS	Remember us always, as we shall remember you.
RAPHAEL	Go with God.
ALL (*answering*)	Go with God.
	(*The Angel departs.*)
TOBIT	Blest be the Lord our God, may His Kingdom be ever blest. He has led us down into death, and has brought us again to life. We shall keep ourselves in truth and in righteousness act and speak, that we may not divide ourselves

	by sin from His holy grace. His promise of healing is sent to Man, who on Earth below his godhood in evil has lost. But the fallen one shall be raised and mercy shown to the sinner; the sorrowful one shall be glad. In a mighty vision I see what those shall know who keep their hearts in faith to God. Today the secret of Man in the Holy Temple is hidden. In the future the City herself, the Holy Jerusalem, shall become the Temple of Man, transformed to his spirit-self. Of precious stones shall be built the form of Man divine. The light of the spirit within shall brighter shine than the Sun. The Temple of Man shall become the eternal City of God.
TOBIAS	My father, you have seen a vision. While your body's eyes were blind, your spirit eyes have learnt to see.
TOBIT	In blindness the vision was born to see afar and ahead what shall fill our life with hope.
TOBIAS	In sorrow we have found joy.
SARA	In sickness we have found healing.
TOBIAS	Because an Angel went with us and opened the eyes of our soul.
TOBIT	May the Lord bless and keep us through all the days of our life, till in the hour of death we find our home with Him.

TOBIAS   And may Raphael, the Archangel,
         be at hand to guard us from evil
         and bring us whole in heart
         to that Home.

THE KING'S INVITATION

The Persons and Spiritual Beings

AN ANGEL
THE KING
ABEL
CAIN
TWO WOMEN
TWO MEN

An Angel (or a group of Angels) begins by making the signs A and O—alpha and omega—then walks the spiral form, inwards and outwards again—indicating thus the sphere of time. In the background is a small altar. On this is a bowl of incense, which is set smoking by the Angel.

ANGEL From alpha to omega,
      from beginning to end,
      from end to beginning,
      stretches the loom
      where the Spirits of Time
      weave through the days,
      through the years and the ages,
      the world's web of existence.
      There is fashioned the pattern
      of life ever-changing,
      epochs rising and waning
      with the coming and going
      of races of men upon Earth.
      The stars in the heights
      are moving and twining
      the colours that thread
      through the pictures of time.
      The gods in the heavens,
      whose thinking is life,
      whose speaking creates,
      brought forth the pattern
      at the birth of the world.
      Then came the devils
      to mingle their meaning
      with the work of the gods,
      distorting their purpose.
      They woke to awareness
      human souls that were dreaming,
      who then made themselves masters
      in their realm of existence
      and wrought into the pattern
      their human intentions,
      till the gods could but little

prevail with their working.
But the Father in Heaven,
whose outspreading arms
bear the World-All within them,
has appointed the hour
when His Word shall go forth
from the heights to the depths of the Earth.

(*The King appears beside the little altar.*)

KING

The hour has come
when the Word of God
shall be heard again upon the Earth,
when the will of God
shall go forth from the heavens
and sound through the world.
In the place where necessities
shape the plan of the present
by the force of the past,
where what has been causes that which is,
shall the beam of grace
from the future fall
and the thoughts divine
from the spirit shall stream
in a golden rain to the hearts of men.

ANGEL (*to King*)

My being is Thine,
my life is of Thee.
My speaking be Thy thinking,
my doing be Thy willing.
At this world hour
when Thy voice from Heaven
shall speak again on Earth
make me Thy messenger.

KING

Thou shalt bear my word
to the ears of men
dear servant of God.
But beware.
When a new urge of life

> from the widths of the world
> invades the Earth region,
> then the air is split open,
> the clouds part asunder,
> the lightning strikes downward,
> around rolls the thunder
> and the storm is released on the land.
> Then one to another
> the Earth dwellers say:
> God's wrath is unloosed.

ANGEL
> They live from Thy bounty, O Lord,
> in a world where Thy forces
> of wisdom and beauty
> are working their wonders.

KING
> They live from my bounty,
> they know life through my working,
> they seek the joys of existence,
> but shrink from its pains.
> They offer me praise
> for the pleasures of living,
> they worship with awe
> the power of my might.
> But their aim is experience,
> the triumph of selfhood
> in every condition—
> content to be creatures,
> to remain as they are.

ANGEL
> Once long ago
> they would hearken to Angels,
> bid them welcome as guests,
> and give heed to their words.
> How changed is it now
> when the presence of Angels
> is hardly regarded,
> or even ignored.

KING
> At the world's creation
> much was bestowed

| | on the children of men.
Through the passing of ages
much has evolved
in their earthly existence.
But much still must grow
if the seed that was sown
in the being of Man
shall bear for the world
the harvest awaited. |

ANGEL With what gifts of the gods
have we not endowed
the children of men?
What has come of these gifts?

KING The hour has come
when the word of God
shall be heard again upon the Earth.
It was not intended
that men should live
by themselves alone,
for themselves alone,
enclosed in the world
that their senses perceive.
It was intended
that in that world
they should waken to selfhood,
should find themselves free.
But what use is freedom
when it is empty.
The Sons of God must converse again
with the sons of man.
The will of God must enter again
the will of Man.

ANGEL Thy thoughts shall be my thoughts,
Thy will shall be my will.

KING The hour is at hand
when the Kingdom of Heaven
shall make known

the new Mystery.
In the sacred place
the tables are spread,
the feast is prepared
and the seat is set
for each chosen guest.
The King's Son is awaiting
His destined bride.
She makes herself ready
to go forth to meet Him.
All things are prepared
for the royal marriage.
Call the guests:
call from the Earth
those who are chosen
to sit at the table
of the Heavenly King.

ANGEL　　Thy behest is my will.

(Screens close round the King. The Angel comes to the two men, Abel and Cain. Abel is asleep before an altar with flowers, fruit and an incense bowl on it. Cain is asleep beside an anvil with tools beside him and objects made of iron.)

Awake and listen, for you are chosen
to be the guests of the Heavenly King.

(Abel wakens and turns to the altar, putting on more incense. When the Angel approaches, he turns away. Cain then wakens and begins to hammer. He ignores the Angel's gesture of invitation.)

ANGEL　　Turn and hear the King's invitation.
To the royal marriage you both are summoned
to be the guests of the Heavenly King.
All is made ready;

you shall feast in abundance.
Leave your earthly concerns
and come to the marriage.
Come into the presence of the Heavenly
   Father.

ABEL   Through the round of the year
my days are filled
with the seemly duties
performed by those
whose lot is to care
for the herds and the flocks,
for pastures and fields,
for seed duly sown
and harvest reaped.
Piously run my days their course
in accord with the life
of the Earth God gave
to men for their home.
Contented am I with the gifts received
from the Sun and the Moon,
from the stars in the heavens,
from the cycle of seasons,
from the passage of years,
from the day to labour,
and the night to rest.
My thanks and my praise
ascend to Heaven,
to Him who dwells there
and gives us life,
in the prayers I pray
in the offerings I bring
each day to this altar
in pious devotion.

CAIN   Through the round of the year
my days are passed
in zealous labour
to fashion the things
that are made with the skill

of human hands,
and conceived through the power
of the human mind.
Mighty talents God gave to Man
to be used to His glory,
and for the joy
men have in creation.
What is dead on Earth—
wood, iron and stone—
is changed to new purpose
and to the wonder
of God's creation
is added the beauty of art.
Men know the divine in themselves
when they fashion
in form and colour,
and they praise God truly
in music that answers
His sounding of the spheres.

ANGEL Do not delay.
Here is my message:
The Father in Heaven sends invitation.
To the marriage feast of the Son
you are bidden. Come away.

ABEL How shall I leave my flocks and herds,
my fields and corn, and my pastures?
Who will care for the sowing and the harvest,
who fill the barns against winter?
Who will provide the household and homestead?
I cannot come.
This land was entrusted to me.
Here I live out my days,
and in my inward soul
there ripens slowly selfhood.
So it is to be a man,
to feel in all experience

the growing new reality
that makes me myself.
This is my lot; to this I cleave,
praising God for my existence.

(*He turns away.*)

ANGEL (*to Caine*) Come away to the marriage.

CAIN My work is unfinished, the iron still hot;
merchants are waiting for my goods
to take them to the distant sea.
Who will finish the work half done?
Who will discover what is not yet invented?
I cannot come.
The human mind has not achieved all it can do.
I work on through the years,
and in my inward soul slowly ripens selfhood.
So it is to be a man,
to feel in all accomplishment
the growing new reality that makes me myself.
I would come with you, but I cannot.
In all beauty created I remember God.

(*He turns back to his work. The Angel makes an imploring gesture, then bows his head and goes away. Cain makes as if to follow him, but then he turns back to his work. As the Angel ascends, the screens are parted to show the King. The Angel stands before the King.*)

ANGEL Thy word went forth to them,
but they would not listen.
The invitation was given
but they would not come.

KING My patience shall for a while endure

and many times the call shall be heard
till the world hour strikes when decision
   is due,
and the crisis comes that shall never
   recur.

(*The screens are closed before the King. The Angel stands with his back to the two men. They go through in mime a struggle with each other, each alternately defending and asserting himself. At last they plant a sword, naked blade upwards between them, and each turns his back on the other. Then each puts on a headdress, the one a bishop's mitre, the other a crown. The Angel goes away.*)

ABEL

I am the leader of men
by the right of the priest.
God has appointed
to all His creatures
their way of existence.
The rocks and the hills
are enthroned in their places.
The plants grow and blossom,
bear fruit and wither.
The beasts move over the land
looking for shelter and food.
To each is accorded his nature.
Likewise to mankind,
the chief among creatures,
is given his labour by day,
his rest until morning,
his food in due season,
and the ordered succession
of each generation.
Praises and thanks
should be offered to Heaven
that men may live out
their fullness of days

The King's Invitation

in pious performance
of their creaturely duties
content to remain
what their Maker has made them.

CAIN

I am the leader of men
by the right of the King.
God has given to men
the use of their reason,
the skill of their hands
and the means to fashion
their existence on Earth.
Man has founded a kingdom
by power of the will.
By their own strength
men shall live for each other.
Let the King of all rule the heavens;
Man shall rule on Earth,
and enjoy his dominion,
for great are the works
that he can perform,
and great his satisfaction
with all his achievements.
Here in this world
men shall be like gods.

(*Enter the Angel in prophet's clothing.*)

ANGEL

How many times in vain
has the messenger of Heaven appeared!
How often have you shut your ears
and turned away your eyes at his coming!
Once again he is sent to you.
Beware, for the time is at hand
when he will come no more.
Yet once again the Heavenly King
invites you to the marriage of the Son,
calls you to learn the new Mystery
by which the sons of men shall be made
companions of the Sons of God.

	Poor creatures, what has become of you? Each turns in hate against the other. Ceaseless struggle now rules your life. Listen to the message from the Father.
ABEL	Leave us to be as we are. We will not hear.
CAIN	We want the kingdom of this world. Return where you belong.
CAIN AND ABEL (*together*)	Go! (*Abel makes a gesture against the Angel. Cain seizes the sword and strikes at the Angel and he falls. The King then appears.*)
KING (*stretching out his hand sternly*)	You have taken the sword. The sword is your doom. (*Both turn away from the King. Cain raises the sword against Abel, who falls; then he falls himself. The King raises the messenger who takes off his prophet's clothes and is an Angel again. Abel and Cain retire.*)
KING	The world hour has struck; the judgment has fallen. They were not worthy who were bidden to the marriage feast of the King. Time and again were they summoned, the great leaders of men, the chiefs of their kind, but they would not come, and never again will they be called. The marriage feast waits, all things are ready. The stars give their forces of life for food to gladden the guests. The bride has adorned herself, and the bridegroom awaits. Go, summon new guests

who will be more willing.
Return no more to the rulers on Earth.
Go instead to the highways
and gather the people
who go up and down on the roadway of life.
They all are invited,
the good and the bad,
the wise and the foolish,
the rich and the poor.
Bring them to the marriage feast.
The doors of the Holy Place are opened.
Human souls of every kind are summoned
to be the guests of the Heavenly King.

ANGEL　They were not worthy who first were invited.
Now to the others, the masses of people
who go up and down on the roadway of life
shall the message be given
from the Kingdom of Heaven.

(The screens are closed before the King. A signpost is set up; one arm says 'Gate of Death', the other 'Gate of Birth'. Two men and two women appear coming from the direction of Birth. They sit down under the signpost.)

1st WOMAN　I have travelled so long on this weary road and still no end is in sight. Life itself has become a burden. Through the years that are gone I have done the work that was given to me with energy and hope. But what is achieved? The results of my work are scarcely to be seen; much is lost, only little remains. To what end? For what do we live? Where are we going?
(wearily)

The road already is dark and empty.

2nd WOMAN: Neither do I see light ahead that would brighten the road. I cannot tell what the end and purpose of this journey should be that we make side by side. I cannot complain that life has not given me much that I wished—a husband, a home and children to rear. But with all my care for daughters and sons, I have seen them grow selfish and anxious for nothing but pleasure and gain. And I am left empty with nothing to guide me to the purpose of living.

1st MAN: We all walk the same road but it seems to lead nowhere. We exist and therefore we are here. There is nothing but to be quiet and decent and to do a good deed now and then. I have tried to take part in the competition for wealth and importance. But what you gain is not worth what you make of yourself in the fight. I have fought in wars and been stunned by the violence and destruction, by the volume of suffering I could neither prevent nor heal. There is nothing left but plodding along the road of life in duty bound.

2nd MAN: We walk the same road but we do not look to the same end. You go meekly, without any purpose, but not I. It is true that I have often failed, but my aims are high. So much is wrong with the way we exist. Surely men should be masters in the world they inhabit using their wit and the skill of their hands for the common good, so that all should enjoy the wealth of the Earth and live out their days in plenty and peace. For this and for people

	like you I have striven. This world could fulfil all the longings and hopes of our hearts if we made it as it should be.
	(*The Angel appears.*)
ANGEL	Hear, you people on Earth, who go up and down on the highway of life, the message from the spirit. The Heavenly King sends invitation to the marriage feast of his Son. Each one is bidden to be his guest, good and bad, wise and foolish, rich and poor. To everyone is opened the door of the Holy Place, where the feast is made ready and the royal servants wait in attendance. Hear the message, answer and come.
1st WOMAN	An invitation is sent to us?
2nd MAN	The door of the Holy Place is open?
2nd WOMAN	The feast is ready and awaits us?
2nd MAN	We shall be guests of the Heavenly King?
ANGEL	You are all elected by invitation to be his guests.
1st WOMAN	I am poor in faith, but I am invited. I will come to the marriage.
1st MAN	I am weak in courage, but I am invited. I will come to the marriage.
2nd WOMAN	I am empty of hope, but I am invited. I

	will come to the marriage.
2nd MAN	Has the hour come at last when I am called to true greatness? I will come to the marriage.
	(*They form into a procession behind the Angel, who leads them off. A screen is removed disclosing an altar, with lighted candles. Some religious music is played. The people return in white garments, except the second man, who looks as before. They take their places before the altar. An Angel appears carrying bread and wine, which he puts on the altar. There is a pause in the music. The King appears. He blesses each of the guests until he comes to the last one (the second man).*)
KING (*to 2nd man*)	My friend, you were bidden to the marriage feast; the door of the Holy Place was opened to you. My servant has led you into the presence of the Sacred Mystery. Where is the garment that the King's guest should wear? How could you enter without the wedding garment?
	(*The man makes a gesture as if he would speak, but he cannot. He covers his eyes and draws back from the King.*)
KING	No one can here remain not clothed in the wedding garment; he must be cast out until in truth he can wear the holy vestment. Go forth, false guest,

from the Holy Place.
My servant will lead you out
and will close the door
upon the marriage feast.

(*The man stumbles backwards and sinks in despair on a step. The King takes bread and wine in his hands from the altar. The Angel comes and puts the screen between the people round the altar and the man outside. The music begins again.*)

ANGEL
(*to the man*)

The wedding garment you could not wear.
The kingly question you could not answer.
At the marriage feast you could not remain.
Outside the door you lie, helpless with grief, speechless with pain.
Fear not the suffering, nor cease your tears;
grow pure with grief, grow wise with pain
that you may find, when
the summons again is heard on the Earth
that you can put on the holy vestment
and take your place at the marriage feast.

MAN Am I not then cast out for ever?

ANGEL The time shall come
when the word of God
shall be heard again on the Earth,
when the will of God
shall speak again
to the hearts of men.
The doors of the Holy Place
shall be opened.
Human souls shall be called
by the King's invitation.

THE GOOD SAMARITAN

The Persons and Spiritual Beings

READER
LIGHT DEVIL
DARK DEVIL
A TRAVELLER
A PRIEST
A LEVITE
THE SAMARITAN
AN INNKEEPER

The Good Samaritan

The parable of the Good Samaritan *(St Luke Chapter 10) is read.*

READER — In every age in Christian times those who pondered on this tale have asked themselves: how shall it be interpreted in terms of our generation? It is timeless, for He told it whose thoughts were beyond time. How can it be told now?

(*Enter two devils.*)

LIGHT DEVIL — Why should he not journey alone to Jericho?

DARK DEVIL — So poor and stupid, how shall he go that dangerous road?

LIGHT DEVIL — He feels a deep longing for Jericho. Why not follow his heart?

DARK DEVIL — He is protected in Jerusalem where law and order prevail.

LIGHT DEVIL — Let him see Jericho and die.
A remnant of Paradise,
a remembrance of Eden,
a place of enchantment
he shall find and enjoy.
He shall bathe in the beauty
of nature unblemished
and himself be renewed
at the fountain of youth.
Hither came Cleopatra
to forget she was mortal,
demeanoured like a goddess,
mocking proudly at death.

DARK DEVIL — Let him remain in Jerusalem
where he belongs.
The priests in authority there
have the situation in hand.

LIGHT DEVIL — Let him break free,

	to be driven by desperate desire.
DARK DEVIL	He will become a prey to fear, losing his sense of direction.
LIGHT DEVIL	To Jericho, to Paradise, he has only to follow me.
DARK DEVIL	When he breaks away from security he will encounter me.

(*Enter a traveller. The light devil leads him onto the road and goes in front beckoning him on, and all around the audience. The dark devil stands behind the traveller.*)

TRAVELLER	Away at last, Jerusalem behind me, Jericho ahead. Such a sense of freedom in heart and in limb! No confining walls, no limiting routine, no cramping obligations and my feet on the open road.
DARK DEVIL	Short-lived freedom! A dark night, a storm, weariness with an empty stomach and you seek the nearest inn, then out with the purse, pass the coins, Mammon wins. You await my service again.
LIGHT DEVIL	Come hurry onwards. The city still lowers behind, but the empty road winds on— liberty lies this way.

(*The devils withdraw behind the rocks.*)

TRAVELLER	It is eerie alone on the road. The hills are closing in, shutting out the view ahead.

Where am I going?
Why am I quite alone?
Why is the sky so dark, so threatening?
When will someone come?
Can anyone face life quite alone?

(*He sits down. The two devils reverse positions. The light devil comes from behind, the dark devil from the front. They fall upon the traveller.*)

LIGHT DEVIL (*pulling the traveller*)	Give!
DARK DEVIL (*pulling in the opposite direction*)	Take!
LIGHT DEVIL	Yield to me.
DARK DEVIL	Wield with me.
TRAVELLER	Help! God help me! Beset on both sides! Oh, what can I do?

(*The dark devil advances on him, he retreats. The light devil pulls him again.*)

TRAVELLER	Help me, O Lord, save me in trouble.
LIGHT DEVIL	Surrender your soul.

(*The light devil snatches the traveller's scarf from him and pushes him towards the dark devil.*)

TRAVELLER	Stop him, he's a thief!
DARK DEVIL	Submit your body.

(*He knocks the traveller down, and takes his money.*)

TRAVELLER	Out of the depths I cry to Thee, save me, O Lord.

(The traveller loses consciousness.)

DARK DEVIL	He shall do nothing without me.
LIGHT DEVIL	He shall think nothing without me.
DARK DEVIL	We have robbed God.
LIGHT DEVIL	God has not denied us.

(They push over the unconscious traveller.)

LIGHT DEVIL   We have robbed God's creature
of what he could not use.
Now his wisdom is mine,
and I am grown great.
I share God's wisdom
and He will perforce share
His dominion with me.

DARK DEVIL   God Himself is robbed.
When He made weakling Man
and set him free to go
beyond His care and rule,
He gave me what I lacked.
A portion of God's will,
I make into my own.
God must henceforth endure
my working in His world.

LIGHT DEVIL   Will God not strike
to reclaim His own?
The child of His hope is slain;
will He revenge Himself?

DARK DEVIL   He took too little care
giving so much to a poor creature,
so stupid that he fell
for every thought of yours.
He cannot touch us now,
when we hold fast together.

LIGHT DEVIL   Hold fast together?

	But I do not admire you;
	my intentions are divine, my principles
	high.
DARK DEVIL	I do not fear you.
	Your fantasies are a dead bore.
	I shall make use of you from time to time.

(*They go off in different directions. Enter a priest, travelling from Jericho towards Jerusalem. He sings the psalm 'I will go unto the house of the Lord'. He sees the traveller lying helpless, but does not at first realize what he is seeing.*)

PRIEST   A clutter on the highway!
This is out of order; a clear road is the rule.

(*He looks closer, then recoils.*)

PRIEST   A man? Wounded? Dead?
Violence has been done here,
here on the highway,
the place of order and law.
Who did this wrong?
They must be brought to justice.
That a public highway
should be a place of danger
is beyond everything.
It must be reported at once.

(*He begins to move on, but looks back from a few paces.*)

Is the poor creature dead?
He neither moves nor answers.
If he is dead, he may lie here
till the body be fetched for burial.
It will be my duty to report
to the authorities in the city.

(*He turns away and then comes back.*)

There are regulations
for the treatment of the corpse.
But should he still breathe,
what is then to be done?
Here I am alone on the road,
my duties in the Temple demand
that I reach the city tonight.
The care of the sick is not for me;
I should not defile myself
by touching blood and dirt—
my Temple duties forbid it.
The law by which I live
makes no provision at all
for a situation such as this.
How can one know what is right to do
when there are no regulations?

(*He hesitates, turns away and comes back again and moves off.*)

If he is dead, all is quite plain.
He makes no sign of life,
he must be dead; it's better so.
I can still reach the Temple
at the correct time.
I shall give official notice
of this shocking affair.

(*Enter a Levite, also going from Jericho to Jerusalem.*)

LEVITE

What a dark stretch of road.
Can it be twilight already?
I started off so early to avoid risks.
If I could only have overtaken
the priest, who went on ahead.
In my position it is impossible
to disobey an order from above.
I try to avoid travelling alone,
but the order came.

The Good Samaritan

(He looks about him and sees the wounded traveller.)

LEVITE
What is this, a disaster?
A wounded man, or dead?
Where are the assailants?
Are they on the look-out for me?

(He moves on, but turns back to look again.)

LEVITE
Perhaps the poor man requires help?
He is beginning to move.
Oh heavens, there is no one here
with authority to give orders.
I cannot decide what to do.
In my position I can't decide.
The man needs help badly,
but I am the wrong person.
I know nothing of wounds;
I might do harm instead of good.
Someone else should take over.

(He looks around.)

There is no one in sight
to turn to for help,
and there are my Temple duties.
I must not fail my obligations.
I do not know this man,
I only happened to be passing.

(The traveller groans.)

Poor man, he suffers.
Such suffering should not be allowed.
Thieves must have set on him;
they ought to have been stopped.
Someone should have prevented it.
God should have prevented it.
How can I put right
what God should have prevented?

(He disappears towards Jerusalem. The traveller groans. From the direction of Jerusalem comes the Samaritan. He looks from side to side apprehensively.)

SAMARITAN

This is the dangerous stretch;
anything might happen here.

(He sees the traveller.)

What foul deed is this?
Have thieves been busy already?

(He kneels beside the traveller.)

He is alive, but scarcely so,
and robbed of all he had.
Poor man, he's in a sorry plight.
His wounds need attention first;
oil, wine, strips of cloth.

(To the traveller.)

Now, drink and drink again,
let nature's life revive your own.
Your goods and gear are lost,
and may never be recovered.
But life is given back to you.
You shall come along with me.
Gently now, drink not too fast.
Life ebbed away, but now the tide
   returns.
Who are you?

(To himself.)

What stranger have I saved
from dying here neglected?
He seems to be from Jerusalem,
so by rule of race and breeding
he is my enemy, and I his.
When he comes again to his senses
will he reject me?

The Good Samaritan

(The traveller groans and the Samaritan gives him another drink. They rest a moment.)

SAMARITAN I shall save his life,
but does he wish it saved?
He has lost everything.
But, with time and care
he may recover strength.
He will have to start his life again
with nothing, nothing but himself.
He may well curse me
who might have let him slip away,
let him escape the trials and the test.
For test it will be to be born again,
to live a second time.
He will build his life again
from what he has in himself.
Only the spirit within can help him then;
he must make his destiny himself.

(The traveller opens his eyes.)

TRAVELLER Who are you?

SAMARITAN He who came and saw you lying helpless.

TRAVELLER Why did you stop?

SAMARITAN I saw a neighbour hard pressed and in trouble.

(The Samaritan lifts him up and they prepare to go on.)

An inn is near at hand where you may rest.

TRAVELLER I took the road to Jericho;
they say it is Paradise.

SAMARITAN The Garden was Paradise once,
now it smells rankly of decay.

	Cleopatra went seeking her lost youth and travelled there anxiously, but what did it avail her?
TRAVELLER	Where is Paradise? Jerusalem is a prison, regulated by duties. Do not take me back.
SAMARITAN	I will take you to the inn. Good people keep it who understand the woes besetting travellers. They will care for you until you travel on again. Your journey has not ended yet. Rest till your strength returns, then start out on the road again.
TRAVELLER	Is it not yet the end?
SAMARITAN	Look, the inn door stands open. Come, here is a resting place.

(*The innkeeper looks out and comes forward to help.*)

INNKEEPER	This is terrible to see, another victim brought so soon. You will be safe enough with us, there are no thieving scoundrels here. Lamps burn in all our rooms and people gather together. The thieves stay out in the dark, which is where they belong.
TRAVELLER	They attacked me from both sides, from behind and from the front.
INNKEEPER (*to traveller*)	It takes much to be alone and come to no harm. You are in poor shape now but we will carry you inside, where you may stay until you are ready to

walk out alone, and go on your journey
once more. But, when you are strong
again, always remember what you owe to
the help of others.

SAMARITAN What I alone could do I did, but more is
needed. I have put him in the care of you
and your household. Here is money for
the present.

(*The innkeeper takes the traveller to a bed.*)

SAMARITAN I will come this way again and pay what
more is due.

INNKEEPER The labourer needs his wage that he can
work tomorrow as today. So we need
payment and we thank you, sir. How did
he come into this plight?

SAMARITAN Travelling towards Jericho
he was attacked by thieves.
He was alone and heedless,
thinking nothing of the journey,
only of the wish to be in Jericho.
Foolishly, he was taken unawares
and overwhelmed from either side.
He was quite unable
to recognize his enemies
or to stand up on his own feet.

INNKEEPER He was another victim
of forces too strong for him
and no one was at hand to help.

SAMARITAN Had I arrived sooner
and rescued him from attack,
he would have been grateful
and gone on none the wiser.
Now his mind will awaken
as he recovers under your care.
He will begin to realize

	what the powers of evil can do, to see that he cannot afford to dream along the road of life.
INNKEEPER	What if, on awakening, he turn against God Himself, who did not save him from suffering and disaster?
SAMARITAN	Does God regard men as happy, ignorant children?
INNKEEPER	The mercy and good that men can show each other, in suffering and trouble, shall be given to him here in my household, that our service to him may be service to God.
SAMARITAN (*counting his money*)	Just enough is left over to finish the journey, with nothing to spare when the innkeeper is paid. All that I can give him will be too little. Later on, I must come this way again.
	(*He puts the money on the table.*)
SAMARITAN (*to the sick traveller*)	Rest well. When the time comes to be off again, go further and fare better.
	(*Exit the Samaritan. The two devils then appear.*)
LIGHT DEVIL	Naturally, we appreciate how much you are doing for him. But, believe me, it's unnecessary when I would do still more.
INNKEEPER	He was given into our care.
LIGHT DEVIL	Would he not be much better in the quiet of my home?

INNKEEPER	It is our custom to care for the sick.
LIGHT DEVIL	But when he gets quite well you will send him on his way again. How could you do otherwise? I intend to provide everything for him; he will fit perfectly into the setting of my household. I regret only that this stranger found him first.
INNKEEPER	He was entrusted to me, I cannot let him go.
LIGHT DEVIL (*angrily*)	You are hindering his best interests; I could have reshaped his life.
	(*Exit the light devil. The dark devil comes forward.*)
DARK DEVIL	Without question he's mine.
INNKEEPER (*turning round to confront the dark devil*)	How did you enter the inn? Not honestly by the front door, that is plain. This sick man is in my care.
DARK DEVIL	Had I known he was not dead, I would not have let him go. But he is to be handed over to me later on.
INNKEEPER	Another stranger has paid for him.
DARK DEVIL	I pay double. My right will be the stronger.
INNKEEPER	But I do not accept. I only need what is required to keep the inn from closing down.
DARK DEVIL	What foolishness! With more means you can expand, increase the number of your guests, take in more unwary fools if you wish.
INNKEEPER	I made a bargain with the stranger and it

	shall be kept.
DARK DEVIL	You are too stupid to know how things should be done. Keep your patient. My time will come again when he closes your door behind him and sets out on his own.
	(*Exit the dark devil.*)
INNKEEPER	No one had in mind the true welfare of this poor man except the stranger.
	(*Exit innkeeper. The Samaritan reappears.*)
SAMARITAN	I find upon reflection that a little more could be spared. The innkeeper will be poorly off.
	(*He puts more money on the table and turns to the traveller.*)
SAMARITAN	The tide has turned, I see, and now you return to life. The hardest moment will be when the defeat has to be faced.
TRAVELLER	Why did you save me? It would have been over by now, and the journey ended.
SAMARITAN	You intended to run away to a quite different place, but you would have run again just as quickly from Jericho, chasing from here to there and back from there to here. But now your journey begins, from this place and this hour.
TRAVELLER	To Jericho? I was going there. You find it useless?
SAMARITAN	Jerusalem to Jericho, Jericho to Jerusalem,

	backwards and forwards, where will you arrive?
TRAVELLER	Shall I stay here?
SAMARITAN	This is only a resting place, the high point where looking ahead the eye penetrates to the distance. It is not a stopping place.
TRAVELLER	I have lost what I had. How should I go forward?
SAMARITAN	You have lost possessions; from within you have lost nothing. You have what you are, you become what you strive after. Look for another road.
TRAVELLER	Where? How?
SAMARITAN	Look into yourself. Behind you is Another. From within look up, beyond you there are others, the light-filled ones. Your destiny is not lived alone. Look for the light that shows you the road.
TRAVELLER (*repeating*)	Look for the light that shows you the road.
SAMARITAN	How did I come to see you, lying so still on the stones? The light in my heart showed me your need.
TRAVELLER	Is there enough light?
SAMARITAN	There is more light than we can use.
TRAVELLER (*getting up*)	There is myself. Just that.

SAMARITAN	If you look into the light
you will know how much light there is.
Look before you set out again.
I shall be back before long;
more money will be owing.
TRAVELLER	Please come back, don't forget.
SAMARITAN	There is still money owing,
I will come back again.
TRAVELLER	My life is yours.
I owe it to you.
SAMARITAN	I give it to you again.
It is yours to take and to shape.
It is yours to make or to break.
You owe it not to me, but to yourself.

THE BODHISATTVA'S WORLD RENUNCIATION

After the Lalitavistara

The Persons and Spiritual Beings

CHORUS OF HEAVENLY BEINGS
ASITA, a hermit
THE KING
CHANDAKA, a charioteer
THE BODHISATTVA, later the Buddha
A VERY OLD MAN
A SICK MAN
A CORPSE
A MONK

SCENE 1

The King is holding audience with the hermit Asita.

ASITA
Forsaking the household life,
I took my way to the forests
that spread green covering
over the king of the mountains.
There many years I lived
devoted to holy contemplation,
observing the custom of hermits.
There were reaped the good results
for which I, wayfaring in Becoming,
had striven through many lives.
There the divine eye was opened,
the power of the god was ripened,
I could send my gaze over the Earth
and through the spheres of the heavens.
I could command powers not human
and move with speed beyond that of feet.
I, Asita, had grown old and holy
in following the duties of the hermit
when a wonder showed itself
to the divine eye within me.

KING
Leaving the shelter of the forest
you have journeyed to my royal city
because of a wonder?

ASITA
Is any light brighter than the Sun?
Does any star outshine the Moon?
A greater light than the Sun at noon,
a brighter star than the Moon at night
was seen before my inner eye,
shining through the heavenly spaces
making visible the dark void of worlds.

KING
What, reverend sir, is the origin
of so great a light?

ASITA
Through the widths of the air

| | music sounded from the spheres
accompanying him as he came,
the splendid one, stepping earthward,
downward, moving in deliberate calm
with six gleaming trunks uplifted,
the young white elephant. |
|---|---|

KING   Such a heavenly portent, holy sir,
            my queen once saw in a dream.

ASITA   The divine eye within me beheld the heavens,
            the garments of the gods were in motion
            as with joy they began to dance
            and to cry aloud through the wide spaces
            the holy name of the Buddha.

KING   How great, reverend sir,
            is your power of divine vision?

ASITA   The eye within me turned from Heaven
            to search through the spaces of Earth
            until the ray of its glance reached India
            and there in the city of Kapilavastu
            in your palace, O King Suddhodana,
            perceived the young prince bearing upon him
            the thirty-two holy signs
            by which the world-hero can be known.
            Therefore am I come from the mountains
            to your city, O King, to see this child.

KING   He shall be brought, holy sir,
            at your request. But at this hour
            he is accustomed to sleep.

ASITA   Such as he require but little sleep.
            It becomes them more to be wakeful.

KING   At your reminder, holy sir,
            he will have wakened.

            (*Exit the King.*)

ASITA	Now shall my days be numbered. My eyes have beheld his coming through whom much salvation is expected.
KING (*returning with the child*)	The prince greets you, reverend sir.
ASITA (*bending in awe over the child*)	In truth the wonder of the world is beheld among us now. All the holy signs are here displayed which mark a world-hero at his birth.

(*Asita begins to weep.*)

KING	Reverend sir, the tears of grief shed at the sight of this child surely foreshadow his woe.
ASITA	The streaming of tears, great King, is not for his sake but mine. Ancient in days am I whose time of departure is near. Not in the flesh shall I witness the hour of the Buddha's becoming. The wheel of the law shall revolve for salvation of gods and men when to Buddhahood he shall attain. As the Udam-bara tree puts forth a blossom at last after long intervals of time, in so rare an hour shall a Buddha appear to succour the world. This prince shall surely be raised to the highest enlightenment and shall save from the ocean of being, from the current of lives recurring, human souls in great number and shall show them that distant shore, the abiding place of salvation.

The Bodhisattva's World Renunciation

But my bodily eyes shall never look
upon the rare jewel of the Buddha.

KING

Joy is in your words of promise, holy sir.
Take the gifts which I shall give
for the prince's sake.

(*A chorus of heavenly beings appears.*)

CHORUS

The sound of coming gods is heard on Earth,
of ceaseless thronging towards the holy child.
The music of the spheres rings in the air
in harmonies sung round him day and night.
The Bodhisattva has come down to men
in light outstreaming through the space of worlds.
The darkness flies away on every side
before the splendour of his dawning light.
Its glory shines on Earth in every part,
stilling all sorrow, healing all disease,
bringing sweet joy instead of bitter hate,
quickening bright hope instead of dark despair.
Its brightness pierces to the underworld,
to Jama's dwelling in the place of shades,
giving release from thirst and hunger's pain
to all dead souls who sojourn in his realm.
Standing upon the mighty lotus flower
which blossomed from the earth to be his throne,
he looks with lion's glance upon the world,
searching through all the spheres of Earth and Heaven.
'I am the first in the wide world,' he cries.

	'This is my final birth. I make an end of birth, old age and death.'
ASITA	Mine eyes have beheld the Bodhisattva through whom salvation is awaited. If in compassion he renounce the world, he shall thereby to Buddhahood attain.
KING	My eyes have seen the signs of greatness, my heart stores up the prophecy of wonders. But why should he renounce the world? He might be lord of kings and kingdoms, through kingship benefiting all the Earth.

SCENE 2

Outside the King's palace.

CHORUS	The anxious murmur of the gods is heard: How fares the Bodhisattva? Where is he? Long years he tarries in his father's house, tasting the princely pleasures in their turn, reared and educated as a king. Coming to manhood, he receives a wife; in female company he dreams his days, with music, song and dancing occupied. O Bodhisattva waken, hear, come forth. All beings wait to hear the holy law. The hour of world-renouncing is at hand. Come forth, prepare for your enlightenment.
CHANDAKA	I sought rebirth in the same hour in which the prince, my master, first saw the light of the world. In the same hour the noble horse,

	Kanthaka, was born for his master's sake. Many times I have driven the chariot when the prince, weary of the palace, sought the delightful paths of the forest. Of late he remains within the gardens hearing the soft music of the women. As the King his father has instructed, they surround him with sweet delights.
CHORUS	Hear, Bodhisattva, in the music's sound, the warning message of the gods themselves. The time has come. Let the immortal stream, the water of salvation, freely flow to all who thirst in Heaven and on Earth. Leave the short joys of youth, that disappear like clouds fast fading in the upper sky.
CHANDAKA	A surfeit of delights are his. But a chill wind of fear blows when the King walks by. The melodies of the harps sound otherwise today. They sing of fading dreams, of going hence.

(*Enter the Bodhisattva.*)

BODHISATTVA	Chandaka, we must drive away; the music sounds of departure. I move through my palaces and seem to take farewell. Above, around, within, the call is heard: Go forth, O Blessed One, go forth.
CHANDAKA	Will you set out for the forest?
BODHISATTVA	We will go forth into the city.
CHANDAKA	The eastern gate is barred.

	The King commanded it so.
BODHISATTVA	Go to my father. Inform him of my desire.
CHORUS	Brief is your life as an image in water, fleeting your days as an echoing sound. Remember the purpose you beheld in becoming. Seek for enlightenment. Now is the time.
CHANDAKA	Warned in a dream of your purpose, the King has made preparation. The eastern gate is open.
BODHISATTVA	Let us go forth.

CHORUS	Now fares the Bodhisattva forth
	through streets adorned and strewn with
	    flowers,
	past houses where the people smile
	to sounds of happy songs and shouts.
	What is this going forth? Where are the
	    poor,
	the old, the sick, the sad, unhappy folk?
	The King has banished them by his
	    decree.
	No sight nor sound of sorrow is allowed.
	The prince sees happiness on every side.
	Dismayed are the gods; they intervene.
	The Bodhisattva must not dream again.

(*A very old man is brought forward by the Chorus and meets the Bodhisattva and the charioteer.*)

BODHISATTVA	Chandaka stop, no further. The city is all gaiety and joy, but here is something strange. Is this a human being. What has befallen him? So bent, so weak, so stricken?

	How can this be?
CHANDAKA	Sir, he is very old.
BODHISATTVA	Old? Have the passing years brought him to this?
CHANDAKA	He has lived on Earth so long that all his limbs are rotted and his senses dimmed.
BODHISATTVA	Does time put such a curse on him alone, or on his kindred, or on us all who are human?
CHANDAKA	On us all, my prince, whose souls are bound to bodies, whose human flesh succumbs to time.
BODHISATTVA	Old age is sorrow, age is suffering, which mortal man must feel. Turn back the chariot. Drive through the eastern gate, back to the land of youth whence we came forth.
CHANDAKA	You met old age against your father's will. He sent the old away from sight.
BODHISATTVA	Can my father's will prevail against oncoming age? Can he, as King, forbid it?
CHANDAKA	No, sire, no king can conquer age.
BODHISATTVA	The gods have sent this sign for my instruction. O mortal man, how sorrowful, how pitiful your mortal fate.
	(They depart.)
CHORUS	The urgent calling of the gods is heard: Come forth, O Blessed One, come forth. Turn from your father's worldly hopes.

> Break the sweet bond to wife and child.
> Renounce the world, to give the world yourself.

(*The Bodhisattva reappears.*)

BODHISATTVA Chandaka, we must drive again.
The world beyond the palace gates
must not remain unknown.
Take the way to the south.

CHANDAKA The city waits for you
and shows a joyful face
as the King commanded.

BODHISATTVA The gods have sent me warnings.
Where are the secret sorrows
concealed when I pass by?

(*The Chorus brings on a sick man in pain.*)

BODHISATTVA Chandaka stop, who is this man?
What has befallen him?
He sighs and moans without relief.

CHANDAKA He is sick and groans with pain,
in the grip of some disease.

BODHISATTVA Is he alone tormented?
Are there others who suffer so?

CHANDAKA Sickness afflicts all mortal men,
some young, some old.

BODHISATTVA Is none exempt from its dangers?

CHANDAKA None, my prince,
neither you, nor I, nor anyone.

BODHISATTVA Who heals the sick?

CHANDAKA Whom the gods favour, to him they send relief.

BODHISATTVA Turn back the chariot. Leave this place of pain.

The Bodhisattva's World Renunciation

(They depart.)

CHORUS The voices of the gods shout louder still:
Come forth, O Blessed One, come forth,
to seek enlightenment.
Renounce the world, to give the world
  yourself.

(The Bodhisattva and Chandaka reappear.)

BODHISATTVA Chandaka, we must go away;
the gods call day and night.
Take the western gate.

CHANDAKA By the will of the gods
you shall be confronted
with the darkest secret.

(A corpse on a bier is brought by the Chorus.)

BODHISATTVA What can this mean?
Who lies so still, alone,
and does not answer?

CHANDAKA He has departed,
leaving wife and child,
father and mother,
not to be seen again
here on the Earth.
he has gone to the other world,
for he is dead.

BODHISATTVA Must all depart at the last?

CHANDAKA All sire, even yourself.

BODHISATTVA The curse of time has struck the world.
Youth fades away,
life is departing hence.
Age threatens, sickness strikes
and death devours at the last.
Turn back again in grief.

(The Bodhisattva sits silent in grief.)

CHORUS
The voices of the gods plead urgently:
Come forth, O Blessed One, at last.
Relinquish grief and seek the holy path.

CHANDAKA
At the northern gate
he now awaits you
whom the gods have sent.

BODHISATTVA
Grief-bringing are the secrets
which the gods have revealed.

(The Chorus appears to show a monk in meditation.)

BODHISATTVA
Who is this stranger?
Wrapped in the quiet of holiness,
strong with the strength of overcoming self,
still with the calm of not requiring.
What is this yellow robe, this empty bowl?
What are these gestures? Whence this dignity?

CHANDAKA
Here stands a monk.
Renouncing senses' lust,
he lives by moral rule,
releasing his soul from hate
and from the worldly passions.
He in peace strives for the spirit,
for his own salvation
and for that of those whose hope
is set on Heaven.

BODHISATTVA
The gods have sent a sign.
In going hence, in world renouncing,
the path begins to the great salvation.
Not for myself alone,
not for my elevation
beyond the mortal fears,

> but for the world salvation,
> for the rescue of captive souls
> I will go forth.
> Let us return,
> the hour of going hence is here.

SCENE 3

Inside the King's palace.

CHORUS
: The music of the gods is heard on Earth.
It whispers on the wind melodiously,
soothing all hearts, inducing quiet sleep.
So silence spreads through every house
    and street.
The gods send silence to the busy world,
because the hour of going hence has
    come,
because the still and holy night begins
wherein the Bodhisattva shall depart.

(The King sleeps; the Bodhisattva stands beside his bed.)

KING (*awakening*)
: Whence comes this light
arousing me at midnight?

BODHISATTVA
: Father, tonight I must depart.
The time for going hence has come
which at my birth has been foretold.
Give me your blessing, father;
let me go with your consent.

KING
: Is this a nightmare or reality?
Beloved son, my only child,
the world has much to give you.
Why resolve on world renunciation?
It was foretold when you were born
that you would a king become,
greater than I or other kings.

	Do not deprive our people of your rule; do not deprive me of my dearest son. Say what you wish, ask of me anything, but do not leave me and my kingdom.
BODHISATTVA	If I requests may make, then I bring you four. If you can grant them, I'll remain. Give me perpetual youth without the pains of age. Give me that beauty that lasts and never fades. Give me good health, secure from all disease. Give me long-lasting life that never ends in death.
KING	The gods themselves do not grant such requests.
BODHISATTVA	Grant me at least this wish, that when I die no urge shall bring me back again to an Earth existence.
KING	I am powerless, my son, to grant such wishes. My affections cling to you, but your soul is departing already, seeking the path of enlightenment. The riddles of existence drive you hence.
BODHISATTVA	Let me go in good will.
KING	My fatherly love would keep you here. Nevertheless, go in peace.

(*The Bodhisattva leaves the King and sees his sleeping wife.*)

BODHISATTVA The bond with the past is broken.
Here she lies, who binds me to the
  present.

Life in the body gave me joy,
but bodily existence ties the soul
to pain, old age and death.
In world renouncing, body overcoming,
the great salvation shall be found.
I say farewell to her in sleep,
and leave the household life,
to take the path of soul release
from ties of Earth existence.

(*Chandaka comes to meet him.*)

CHANDAKA The horse, Kanthaka, is prepared
as you instructed me.
What purpose has this going forth
in secret in the night?

BODHISATTVA I must depart, Chandaka.
Come with me through the darkness
until I lay aside my princely garments.
Then you shall take the empty clothing
and show them to my father.

CHANDAKA My prince, consider. You are young,
you taste the joys of Earth existence.
World renunciation comes with age.

BODHISATTVA Those joys dissolve like clouds
and fade like dreams.
They are but illusions,
changing from hour to hour.
My soul is seeking strength
to cross emotions' moving waves,
to bear the salty thirst of longing,
to overcome the snake of instinct.

CHANDAKA Is salvation only in rejecting,
in renouncing what gives joy
to the soul inhabiting the body?

BODHISATTVA The soul has changed direction.
Drawn Earthward by the senses,

shut up in the body of flesh,
the soul no longer sees the divine,
or hears the music of the spheres,
or knows the presence of God.
The soul has lost the beginning
and shall return by the path of
   renunciation.
Such is the way of world salvation.

CHANDAKA   Is there no other way?

(*The Bodhisattva is silent, but departs, beckoning to Chandaka to follow.*)

CHANDAKA   Can only the away-going path
lead to enlightenment?

(*Chandaka follows without receiving an answer.*)

CHORUS   The jubilation of the gods is heard,
the great salvation is beginning,
the act of world renunciation is
   performed,
the hour of going forth has come,
the Bodhisattva seeks enlightenment.
Rejoice inhabitants of Earth and Heaven,
the Blessed One shall rise to Buddhahood
to save the many anxious human souls
from drowning in the sea of lives repeated
and lead them to the quiet shores beyond,
to world salvation in eternity.

(*Chandaka returns.*)

CHANDAKA   He has departed; I return alone,
bringing the empty garments.
The purpose of my life is over.

(*Enter the King.*)

KING   The prince's wife asks for him.
What has become of him, Chandaka?

The Bodhisattva's World Renunciation

(Chandaka silently holds out the garments.)

CHANDAKA His head is shorn.
He wears the yellow robe.

KING The act of world renunciation is performed.
Our life is turned to grief, hers, yours and mine.

CHORUS The jubilation of the gods is heard.
They shake the solid earth with joy
and fill the air with scents of Paradise.
They sing of world salvation and of hope.
The Bodhisattva has at last gone forth.

ST FRANCIS CONVERTS THE ROBBERS

After the Fioretti *or* Little Flowers of St Francis

The Persons and Spiritual Beings

CHORUS OF ANGELS
A BEGGAR (a holy man in disguise)
FRANCIS
MOTHER OF FRANCIS
TWO ROBBERS—
  1st ROBBER
  2nd ROBBER (later a FRIAR)
ROBBERS' VICTIM
FRIAR ANGELO
AN ANGEL

SCENE 1

CHORUS OF ANGELS
O Lord most high,
be Thou praised and glorified.
Out of Thy goodness Thou sendest him
to be the messenger of Thy compassion.
Not to the great and mighty he comes,
nor to those endowed with great learning,
but to the poor and lowly,
to the foolish, and humble in heart,
to those who are wise in the ways of
    poverty,
who are strong to endure tribulation.

(*Enter a holy man disguised as a beggar.*)

BEGGAR
He is born a babe unnoticed
in the household of a merchant.
In the pious heart of his mother
a dream of his greatness lives,
while his father hopes for a son
to be a better merchant than himself.
The child's soul will be confused
by so much dreaming.
A portent shall be sent to give him
    strength.

(*The beggar knocks on a door.*)

Alms for the love of God,
alms for sweet Jesus' sake
who was born in a stable.

(*The mother appears with the child Francis in her arms.*)

MOTHER
Here are alms for His sweet sake
who was born in a stable.

BEGGAR
God's blessing be upon you
and upon your little child.

MOTHER
Pray for him, good sir.

| | You beg food from me
            but I beg prayers from you.
            Pray for him that he may grow
            to follow God's will. |
|----------|---|
| BEGGAR | That will I do, sweet lady,
            for he has a great calling. |
| MOTHER | Good sir, who are you?
            You come as a stranger
            and know my closest secret.
            Before his birth I saw in a dream
            that he must be born in a stable,
            that he might follow the One,
            who had nowhere to lay His head.
            When my hour came I left home
            and sought a barn by the road,
            that he might be born in the straw,
            poor and homeless as the Child Jesus. |
| BEGGAR | You did well to obey the dream. |
| MOTHER | My husband was away from home.
            He must never hear of this.
            He has other ambitions,
            hoping for a quick and clever son,
            able to gain money and spend it,
            to make our name known in Assisi. |
| BEGGAR | He is born to a great decision,
            to choose between two destinies,
            between the father's worldly ambition
            and the mother's inner vision;
            between the pomp of wealth and pride
            and the humble ways of poverty;
            between arrogant authority
            and the strength that comes from compassion;
            between temporal desires
            and the lasting joys of Paradise. |
| MOTHER | Must the choice be made? |

St Francis Converts the Robbers

Is there no other way?

BEGGAR He will encounter the choice
between the prince of this world
and our Master, Jesus Christ.
He will lead the souls of men
to valorous deeds in battle
or to loving acts of compassion.
But before he passed the gate of birth
in the illumination of the spirit,
he had already decided
for the sake of Christian compassion
to walk the path of poverty,
to choose obedience and chastity,
that the pattern of His Master,
the image of Jesus, shine
in his words and in his deeds.

MOTHER Shall he become a monk?

BROTHER He is born to be the brother
of the poor and the unfortunate,
of the sick and the outcast,
and of all God's creatures
on whom the great Sun shines.

MOTHER Pray for him and for me,
that we may be protected from the Evil
One.

BEGGAR May God's blessing shine upon you,
now and in the time to come.

(The beggar steps back into the Chorus.)

CHORUS OF ANGELS O Lord most high,
look on Thy servant Francis
and keep him from evil temptations.
Thou hast sent him where the Devil's
snares shall beset him at every step.
Thou hast given him a god-fearing
mother

but a father full of worldly pride.
Let him remember the holy resolve
and the delight in divine compassion
which he knew before he came to Earth.
O Lord, save him from evil
and make him to be one of Thy saints.

SCENE 2

Francis has started out on a journey away from Assisi.

FRANCIS	It is already evening;
	I have come so short a way
	since I set out this morning,
	but I can go no further tonight.
	Apulia is yet a long way off.
	At starting I was hindered
	by that unfortunate knight,
	an old friend in a sorry state,
	so ill clad that he was ashamed
	to show himself for service at court.
	Then, returning for more clothing
	after my friend had donned my own,
	my mother delayed me.
	She knows of my dream,
	which sends me off to the wars,
	but she is loath to see me a knight-at-arms.
	(*He sits down to prepare for sleep.*)
CHORUS OF ANGELS	Listen, Francis, listen.
FRANCIS	Voices, whose are they?
CHORUS OF ANGELS	Listen, Francis, listen.

St Francis Converts the Robbers

FRANCIS	So I have heard in dreams. Speak on, you voices, speak. I am ready to listen.
CHORUS OF ANGELS	Francis, do take care how you apprehend the Mysteries shown to you by divine mercy.
FRANCIS	A dream was shown to me of a fair and great palace, the walls hung with pieces of armour which I should take and put on. Each one bore the cross of Christ. Because of this portent, I shall take up the soldier's life.
CHORUS OF ANGELS	Think, Francis, once more. Whom should you rather serve, the lord or the servant, the rich man or the poor?
FRANCIS	Surely the lord, or the rich man.
CHORUS OF ANGELS	Why leave the lord for the servant, the rich God for a poor mortal?
FRANCIS	God is indeed the greatest Lord that a poor mortal can serve. Why should I obey commands from a man mortal as I, if I may receive behests from God? I thought in truth that the dream was a sign from on high, exhorting me to valorous deeds. Give me counsel. What shall I do?
CHORUS OF ANGELS	Interpret the dream aright. Put on the spiritual armour that your soul may be valorous to withstand the powers of evil and, by the strength of compassion, to rescue the sick and the sinful.

	Return and await God's sign.
FRANCIS	How may I find God's armour against the enticements of the Devil?
CHORUS OF ANGELS	In ardent prayer you will find it.
FRANCIS	I will return at your bidding.

(*Exit Francis.*)

CHORUS OF ANGELS	O Lord most high, send counsel to Thy servant. Show him the power of the spirit to perform the deeds of compassion in which Christ works on the Earth.

(*Re-enter Francis with his mother.*)

FRANCIS	The dream that spoke of battles was a sign of spiritual fight. I must turn from worldly conceit to the humble life of prayer.
MOTHER	My son, the soldier wounds, but he who prays can heal.
FRANCIS	God in His mercy warned me to engage in wars of the spirit. Therefore I am come.
MOTHER	Praise be to the divine mercy that leads you along the path which was foretold at your birth. But your father, alas, will rage in fury when he hears about your resolve.
FRANCIS	Come rage, come fury, come pain of parting, the resolve is taken.
MOTHER	What shall become of you? What will you do?

St Francis Converts the Robbers

FRANCIS
: I will become as poor
as I was at the hour of birth.
I will obey my Master
as my hand obeys my will.
I will live as chastely
as He whom I strive to follow.

MOTHER
: How may you do so
and remain in the world?

FRANCIS
: My occupation shall be prayer
until a further sign is sent.

MOTHER
: Your father is within.
I will prepare him for this change.

(*Exit mother.*)

CHORUS OF ANGELS
: Francis, consider.
Let your heart prepare
for want and homelessness.

FRANCIS
: My soul vows to abstain
from all that binds it to the Earth,
from ties to hearth and home,
from human loves and duties
and from all temporal things.
My soul encounters loneliness.

CHORUS OF ANGELS
: Francis, consider.
Let your heart prepare
for the hard yoke of obedience.

FRANCIS
: My soul vows to obey
the bidding of the spirit's voice.
My own will surrenders
to inspiration from above.
Why be myself, when through my will
the purposes of Jesus work in me.
My soul seeks sacrifice.

CHORUS OF ANGELS
: Francis, consider.
Let your heart prepare

	for grief and disappointment.
FRANCIS	My soul vows to attain to freedom from the power of flesh. My heart turns Heavenward, seeking the light of thought and warmth of feeling from above, to penetrate my words and deeds. My soul finds consolation.
	(*His mother re-enters.*)
MOTHER	My son, your father swears to haul you off before the bishop, there to deprive you of your wealth and share in the inheritance. He casts you from him publicly. My son, consider, it is not too late; he still could be appeased.
FRANCIS	What do you wish of me?
MOTHER	You were intended to become the brother of the poor and helpless ones, of the sick, and of the outcast too. But must you be yourself cast out?
FRANCIS	I will go forth myself and leave my father's house, casting the very clothing from me that came of his providing. No outcast I, but one who of himself casts off what this world gives. I called him father once on Earth. Henceforth, I boldly say: 'Our Father, who art in Heaven.' To Him I now surrender to be His faithful son forthwith. Farewell.
MOTHER	Farewell, dear son, God keep you.
FRANCIS	I run to meet my earthly father

before the bishop's throne.
New born to God, new life begins.

(*They depart in opposite directions.*)

SCENE 3

Two robbers are bending over the body of their victim.

1st ROBBER	He seems not to breathe, you hit much too hard.
2nd ROBBER	Skulls are like rock in Monte Casale. Look again.
1st ROBBER	It is as we feared. The townsfolk will come in a pack to have our blood. I swear we never meant to kill.
2nd ROBBER	There was no need before, but he held too fast to his purse, and there was little enough in it too. We have made a bad bargain.
1st ROBBER	Footsteps! God have mercy! Vengeance comes without delay.

(*They both run away, but the second one does not go far, and conceals himself. Friar Angelo comes by singing a psalm.*)

FRIAR ANGELO A dead man! God rest his soul!

(*He looks closer.*)

Praise be to God! A miracle!
He breathes again. In my cell
his hurts shall be bound up.

(*He carries off the victim. The robbers then return.*)

2nd ROBBER	No need to dig a grave. The friars will care for the burial.
1st ROBBER	What will become of us? No one will sell us bread now, even for a great sum, and we have little. I long for the old honest life, fearing only the Devil and his minions.
2nd ROBBER	And now they are afraid and call us devils, and so we are. You without intention, I because my estates were stolen. 'Tis a devil-ridden world, devoid of justice; we fend for ourselves.
1st ROBBER	There was I, praying loud, calling on St Christopher in the dark, when the band of robbers met me, forcing me to go with them. Alas, my poor damned soul!
2nd ROBBER	Alas, my poor empty stomach. We are robbers like to become beggars. What says your pour soul to that?
1st ROBBER	Beggars? Who will give bread to us?
2nd ROBBER	The holy friars maybe.
1st ROBBER	The friars? God forbid! How can we beg from them? They live from alms themselves.
2nd ROBBER	Then they shall give alms to us. It befits their piety to do so.
	(*They go on to where Friar Angelo appears at the door of his cell. The robbers approach. The second walks up to the friar, takes his bowl and holds it out towards him.*)
2nd ROBBER	Alms, holy friar, of your goodness.

1st ROBBER   Have mercy for the love of God,
                   unfortunate starvelings are we.

FRIAR ANGELO   Who are you? God forbid!
                   You are the robbers of ill fame,
                   who beset the people of Monte Casale.
                   Begone from here.

2nd ROBBER   We are without food and drink.
                   You receive alms. Now give in God's name.

1st ROBBER   Have pity on our need.
                   God have mercy on our souls.

FRIAR ANGELO   Robbers and manslayers,
                   not ashamed to steal from others,
                   would you also devour
                   the alms given to God's servants?
                   You are not worthy to walk the Earth,
                   having reverence for neither God nor man,
                   forgetting how you were created.
                   Begone! Come here no more.

1st ROBBER   He damns us in God's name.
                   Oh my poor damned soul,
                   it shall be thrown into Hell.
                   The holy friar condemns me,
                   as God will at the Judgment.

2nd ROBBER   What kind of holiness is yours?
                   You hold out the begging bowl,
                   hard-working folk fill it full,
                   but you have no mercy for us.
                   You are wrapped in a cloak of holiness
                   to keep yourself from evil.
                   You cast us beggars from you
                   into temptation and darkness.
                   Your holiness is for yourself.

FRIAR ANGELO   You struck a man not long since,

	with intent to rob and kill. By the grace of God, and my pity, he has been saved from death. You are murderers beyond redemption. Unrepentant, you shall be judged, not by Man, but by God Himself. Depart with all speed.
1st ROBBER	By the justice of God we are condemned already. Is there no mercy for sinners?
2nd ROBBER	Who are you to speak for God, puffing yourself up with holiness?

(*They go off in anger.*)

FRIAR ANGELO	They forget God in their deeds but His name is much on their lips.

(*Enter Francis, carrying bread and wine.*)

FRANCIS	Look, Friar Angelo, how much we have received by the great goodness of God from the hands of honest men.
FRIAR ANGELO	The Lord be praised indeed for we have much need of food; a wounded man is our guest who lately fell among robbers.
FRANCIS	He shall share our all.
FRIAR ANGELO	Those irreverent murderers came here to beg from us. But I showed them plainly the blackness of their sin, sending them off, as is right.
FRANCIS	Sinners are not drawn to God by harsh reproof—quite otherwise. They are better led by gentleness. The whole need not a physician

	but those who are sick. Thus said He who we follow as our Master. Against charity you have acted, against His gospel have you spoken. You owe my holy obedience. I command you to take bread and wine, to seek through valley and over hill, until you find those robbers. Give them this food from me. Humbly confess your fault and entreat them heartily to cease their evil deeds.
FRIAR ANGELO (*kneeling*)	Holy obedience constrains me, reverend father. I will pray for them.
	(*Angelo meets the robbers, who are sitting sullenly with their heads in their hands. He kneels before them.*)
FRIAR ANGELO	Take the alms refused before. Friar Francis sends bread and wine because of holy compassion, and commands me here to confess cruelty of deed and word. If you will turn towards God, giving up your evil ways, the friars will provide for you, not once, but constantly.
2nd ROBBER (*to 1st robber*)	What do you say?
1st ROBBER	He has brought food and drink.
FRIAR ANGELO	Friar Francis sends his promise, and will pray for you.
	(*He departs and the robbers begin the meal. The 1st robber eats greedily and then begins to weep.*)

1st ROBBER	Wretched creatures are we, here in this life outlaws, sure later of torment in Hell.
2nd ROBBER	We have robbed without pity, without fear of God or man. We deserved vengeance, but the friar sent a free gift and promised more than we asked.
1st ROBBER	Did you hear him confess that he had cruelly used us?
2nd ROBBER	He had rebuked us rightly, but this action so gentle has unfrozen my heart. Remorse coming untimely how bitter it is!
1st ROBBER	If we could only confess our sin.
2nd ROBBER	Bitter is repentance too late.
1st ROBBER	Fearful is the wrath of God.
2nd ROBBER	Is there an escape from evil?
1st ROBBER	Is there mercy for sin?
2nd ROBBER	What must we do?
1st ROBBER	Alas, what can we do?
2nd ROBBER	Have the friars medicine for sin as much as food for the body?
1st ROBBER	Are their prayers heard in Heaven?
2nd ROBBER	We will go to Friar Francis.
	(*They depart.*)
CHORUS OF ANGELS	O Saviour of sinners, be praised for Francis, Thy servant, who is the messenger of Thy compassion. He is fearless before the wicked,

St Francis Converts the Robbers

who have fallen into temptation.
He brings help to them that suffer
and rescues evildoers from sin.

(*Francis appears. The robbers run to meet him, the first kneeling, the second holding out his hands.*)

1st ROBBER
Our sins burden us sorely.
Can we find the mercy of God?

2nd ROBBER
Our own snare entangles us.
Show us what we should do.

FRANCIS
God's mercy is boundless.
Were the sins beyond counting
God's mercy would still be enough.
The apostle Paul has said:
Into this world came Christ
for the saving of sinners;
He does not abhor the sinner
but looks with compassion upon him
who has fallen a prey to the Devil.

1st ROBBER
Then we are not condemned?

2nd ROBBER
How may the compassion of Christ
work upon us now?

FRANCIS
The powers of evil seized you,
they robbed your souls of grace,
they left you in fear of God
and hate of your fellow men.
Abjure the power of devils
and cease to do their work.

ROBBERS
We abjure the power of devils
and vow to do no evil.

FRANCIS
The body must suffer pain
and the dread of foul disease.
It is doomed to age and death.
The soul is destined for Heaven

	but in danger of falling to Hell. Look to the soul's salvation and leave the concerns of life that bring mere temporal gain. Turn away and strive towards Heaven.
1st ROBBER	Let us stay in your company, lest we fall again into evil.
2nd ROBBER	Show us the way of salvation and teach us to walk therein.
FRANCIS	Through Christ is given salvation to erring human souls. He reigned with the Father in Heaven, but the bitter need of mankind drew Him downwards to the Earth. In compassion He walked among men, tending and healing the sick. With the strength of compassion He died and overcame death on the Cross. In the light of compassion He leads human souls on the path towards God.
ROBBERS	Let us share in divine compassion.
FRANCIS	Our company of friars join for this same purpose together.
ROBBERS	We would follow Him likewise.
FRANCIS	Come with me.
CHORUS OF ANGELS	O blessed Master, be praised for Francis, Thy servant, who shows Thy compassion to sinners. They were sons of eternal wrath who now are cleansed by repentance and seek the way of salvation.

(*There is a pause. The 1st robber sinks to the ground.*)

But the strength of one is failing,

death of body seizes him,
we receive his departing soul
and guide him towards Paradise.
He shall taste the joys of Heaven
in the company of saints.

(*They receive the 1st robber and lead him away.*)

SCENE 4

The 2nd robber, now a friar, is walking up and down in contemplation.

CHORUS OF ANGELS
O merciful Lord,
look on this soul with compassion:
once a cruel thief, now a penitent,
zealous in prayer and in fasting,
persevering in acts of contrition,
weary in body and faint in heart.

FRIAR
The guilt of sin oppresses me.
My soul seeks holiness,
but what avails against the guilt?
Ceaseless repentance, but so little hope.

(*He sits, and goes to sleep. An Angel from the Chorus approaches him.*)

ANGEL
Come with me, foolish friar;
I am sent to show you the way.

FRIAR
To show me the way to redemption?

ANGEL
You crouch in the bog of repentance.
Arise, and follow me.

FRIAR
You are a messenger from Heaven.
I will go with you.

(*The Angel leads him to a steep place and pushes him; he falls with a cry of fear.*)

CHORUS OF ANGELS	Take heed, good soul, you are cast down to rise again with inner strength. Stand upright.
FRIAR	Broken to pieces and shattered am I. Can this be Angels' work? Where am I? Who am I?
ANGEL	Rise up. A greater journey is before you.
FRIAR	Foolish and cruel guide, I am dashed to pieces.
ANGEL (*touching him*)	You have prayed to find the way to redemption. Rise up and come.
FRIAR	Your touch gives me strength. But where are we going now?
CHORUS OF ANGELS	Take heed, good soul, this plain bestrewn with stones, with thorns and briars, you must cross. The mind awakes in pain to learn what foolishly it would not see.
ANGEL	Cross on your naked feet, and do not heed the pain.
FRIAR (*walking painfully*)	Why is this Angel sent to bring such grief to me?
CHORUS OF ANGELS	Beware, good soul, the fiery furnace lies ahead through which you next must pass. The flames will purify the heart from dross of greed and fear.
ANGEL	Enter boldly in.
FRIAR	After the cruel plain a fiery furnace for repose? Fire consumes and melts me till I do not know myself.

(The Angel touches him.)

ANGEL
Be strong and whole.
Three trials are safely past.
Have courage to rise up again.

FRIAR
I thought I had repented earnestly.
But true and sharp repentance
I learn in threefold form to know.
Where shall I find redemption?

ANGEL
See there a bridge,
over the stormy water spanned.
Will you cross it?

FRIAR
If it leads beyond repentance
at last to true redemption
I will go on.

ANGEL
A dreadful river flows beneath;
dragons and serpents there abound,
waiting for victims to devour.
The bridge is frail and weak,
without a rail or foothold sure.
But cross you must, at any cost.

FRIAR
How may I do so?

ANGEL
Follow me, and place your feet
where I place mine.

FRIAR
I follow.

(The Angel walks on. The friar follows slowly. In the middle of the bridge the Angel spreads wings and flies up to a peak, behind which a shining door appears.)

FRIAR
Stop! Help!
Though you be a messenger from Heaven
it is a poor trick to leave me now.

CHORUS OF ANGELS
Be strong, good soul.
The dragon jaws gape wide below.

> The winged guide is far beyond.
> Return you cannot.
> Mercy Divine, look down
> upon this hapless soul.

(*The friar kneels and clasps the bridge.*)

FRIAR Unto thee, O Lord, I commend my soul
that I be saved from the jaws of fiends.

CHORUS OF ANGELS Have mercy upon him, O Lord,
and show him Thy salvation.

(*He kneels for a time, then raises his head.*)

FRIAR None less than an Archangel
could rescue me from such danger.
But no messenger comes.
There is no divine intervention.
Is my prayer unheard?
What stirs on my back,
growing and spreading?
Wings! Wings like an Angel's!
Praise be to God, who heard me
and sent me wings to fly from danger.

(*He starts to fly; the wings fail him and he falls back on the bridge.*)

FRIAR O Lord, behold my plight.
Send me again Thy succour.

CHORUS OF ANGELS Thou art a very present help in trouble,
O Lord, our God and our Redeemer.

FRIAR I feel the wings grow stronger.
But patience, I was too hasty.
Now, away! Off, fiends! I outsoar you.

(*He flutters a little way, but falls back on the bridge.*)

FRIAR Oh foolish haste! What rash impatience!
Upholding grace has let me fall;

	the fiends deride and mock me. But I will pray again to God, who does not weary of my prayers.
CHORUS OF ANGELS	O Lord, behold his need. Let not his soul be seized by these devouring fiends.
FRIAR	The wings are stirring. Patience, and yet more patience. Haste shall not mar their growth.
CHORUS OF ANGELS	Be thou praised, Mercy Divine, for Thy goodness to Thy servant. At the third time he shall rise from the mocking jaws of fiends.
FRIAR	The wings grow mightily. But patience. Now, it is time! They bear me upwards from the bridge.
CHORUS OF ANGELS	Rise up, good soul, approach the shining gate of Heaven. The fiends shall howl for you in vain. The grace of God shall lift you up from depths of sin to heights of light.
ANGEL	So, Friar, you have come at last.
FRIAR	But not by any help of yours. You left me halfway through. By might of God within myself I rose on wings to Heaven's gate.
ANGEL	Did you not earnestly enquire for the way of redemption? Only within yourself is the strength to go that way. You are not redeemed by me, but, with God's help, by yourself.
FRANCIS	Good friar, before ye enter in look back along the way you came.

An outcast once, you cast yourself
beyond the reach of temporal joys,
to join the company of friars
who only live for holiness.
Repentance so required it.
But now redemption's Mystery
is known to you, though still in dreams.
Awaken again to life on Earth
and cease to fear its evil threat.
A holy treasure lies hidden there,
which Christ Himself reveals to those
who seek redemption undismayed
by fierce temptation, guilt and sin.
Do not desire escape to Heaven
but learn to overcome on Earth.
Man's soul shall rise again in Christ.

FRIAR

By holy obedience, father,
I leave the blessed dream of Heaven
and turn again to Earth.

CHORUS OF
ANGELS

O blessed Saviour,
be thou praised and glorified
for the wisdom of Thy servant Francis.
Thou hast made him the messenger of
   Thy compassion
to bring healing to sick and sinful men,
to be the brother of all humble creatures.
Thou hast made him a guide to human
   souls
who seek the way of redemption.
Thou hast made known to him the joys of
   Heaven
and revealed at last the secret of the
   Earth.
Praise to the Lord. Praise to the Divine
   Mercy.

THE PRODIGAL SON

Persons, Spiritual Beings and Creatures

TWO SERVANTS
ELDER SON
FATHER
YOUNGER SON
SILENT BROTHER FIGURE
LIGHT DEVIL
DARK DEVIL
A GNOME
A SYLPH
AN UNDINE
A SALAMANDER
PIGS

SCENE 1

At the entrance to a house within a courtyard and built in the style and proportions used by Fra Angelico, two servants appear. Their costumes are of a simple style.

1st SERVANT   Where is the master of the house?
He was always here
at the usual time
until now—

2nd SERVANT   Our fellow servants
will have gone to the fields
and begun the day's work.
But we must wait here
to receive our instructions.

1st SERVANT   Is something new in the air?

2nd SERVANT   The master went with heavy step
in recent days.

1st SERVANT   Can you foresee his plans?

2nd SERVANT   His mind is as wide
as his great estates
I see with a servant's eye.

1st SERVANT   Far stretch the lands
of which he is the lord
whom we serve through the seasons,
so far that their bounds
I have never yet seen.

2nd SERVANT   To strange places afar
have I travelled with him
when he was concerned
to know for himself
the state of his lands.
To the utmost limit
we never came.

1st SERVANT   He keeps his wealth wisely

| | and looks for the thriving
of all in his care.
His rule is well ordered,
his law firm established
in great things and small. |
|---|---|
| 2nd SERVANT | He knows well the strength
of order maintained
of laws rightly kept.
But he understands more
the flash of new thought,
the aim beyond plan,
the purpose unknown. |
| 1st SERVANT | Justice and right
are upheld by his hand.
What he ordains
his servants perform. |
| 2nd SERVANT | Mercy and grace
he freely can give.
More he performs
than his servants foresee. |

(*The elder son enters.*)

| ELDER SON | Where is my Father?
He will surely come with me
away to the fields. |
|---|---|
| SERVANTS | We wait for him to come,
He is still within doors. |
| ELDER SON | Why such delay?
The usual hour is past
when the work of the day should begin.
Enquire when he comes. |

(*1st servant goes out.*)

| ELDER SON
(*to 2nd servant*) | See how high the Sun climbs
on his daily path and we are still idle. |
|---|---|

(*The servant returns with the Father.*)

FATHER	The day brings forth the glory of God; the Sun declares it through the heavens. Star unto star in answer calls and from the depths sounds back the echo. Blest be the light of day for creation. Blest be the life that quickens the creatures. Blest be the labour, my son, of your strength.
ELDER SON	Blest be the day for you my Father. The time for work has come. The servants wait and we should go.
FATHER	What shall be done today?
ELDER SON	Wide are the fields of the stars where the world seeds quicken that are sown in the heavens. Many are the servants sent to till those fields with care and each in his skill and strength is fit for the work he plies. There the harvest is grown that is reaped for the sake of the world. There creation continues that the universe may endure. There life is born out of life that the works of God may not cease. Shall not the elder son go up and down in the fields and with the voice of the Father speak to the servants at work? Who shall care for the order and working of all things but he?

(*Chorus of servants in question and answer.*)

1st SERVANT	What shall the harvest be that is reaped in the fields of the Moon?

2nd SERVANT	When the wisdom of God is sown in the fields of the Moon the power to give form is brought forth that works in the world's becoming.
1st SERVANT	What shall the harvest be that is reaped in Mercury's fields?
2nd SERVANT	When the wisdom of God is sown in Mercury's fields the power to heal is brought forth that flows where sickness is wielding.
1st SERVANT	What shall the harvest be that is reaped in the fields of Venus?
2nd SERVANT	When the wisdom of God is sown in the fields of Venus the power of love is brought forth that one to the other attracts.
1st SERVANT	What shall the harvest be that is sown in the fields of the Sun?
2nd SERVANT	When the wisdom of God is sown in the fields of the Sun, the glory of light is brought forth that in beauty creates through the world.
1st SERVANT	What shall the harvest be that is sown in the fields of Mars?
2nd SERVANT	When the wisdom of God is sown in the fields of Mars the power to speak is brought forth that utters the word from within.
1st SERVANT	What shall the harvest be that is sown in Jupiter's fields?
2nd SERVANT	When the wisdom of God is sown in Jupiter's fields the power of thought is brought forth

that gives to the world its meaning.

1st SERVANT
What shall the harvest be
that is sown in Saturn's fields?

2nd SERVANT
When the wisdom of God
is sown in Saturn's fields
recollection within is brought forth
that lets inwardness live in the world.

ELDER SON
Who shall watch the harvest?
Who shall measure the corn?
Who shall care for the keeping
and the rightful sharing
of the gathered grain?
Who but the son and the Father
shall give heed to the whole?

FATHER
My son, you are regent
through the extent of my lands.
You are sent to uphold
the rule of right order
and the might of my law.

ELDER SON
To this I am bound, my Father,
by the whole will of my nature.
Let us go at once to the fields.
Or must I go in your stead?

FATHER
Go alone, my son.
The servants will hear
that you speak with my voice.
I must stay here
for the sake of your brother.
He is young and begins to ask
what shall become of him.

ELDER SON
Shall he not go with me
and learn the care of your lands?

FATHER
To each of my sons is due
his share in our wealth,
his task in the whole

	and his way of life. You have what is yours. Go now my son, and may your toil be blest and the harvest thrive.
ELDER SON	As you will, my Father. At evening I shall be here again.
	(He goes away. The younger son comes in.)
YOUNGER SON	He strides on ahead and will not turn at my call. There is no time to wait, I must be ready and off. He should have stayed for me.
FATHER	He cannot know that you will go before evening. He could not imagine a wish like that you uttered today. You have outgrown boyhood and are filled with desire to find the unknown. When your brother reached manhood he found contentment in the daily cares of our estates. Such work could be yours.
YOUNGER SON	It is enough, my Father, that one of your sons will stay at your side to uphold in all things your order and farseeing rule. But I long to leave home and the shelter of your domain, to go where my endeavour will shape my way of existence. Set me free to depart.
FATHER	You are weary of home, my son, eager to be away,

	longing for the new world beyond the old boundaries. What do you hope for there? For liberty not known within my ordered domain? My son, you are seeking danger.
YOUNGER SON	Shall the son be restrained by the fears of the father?
FATHER	Not from fear of disaster have I given my warning, but to remind you that you seek without understanding that which you cannot know. But seek you shall and alone.
YOUNGER SON	May I go with your good will?
FATHER	It must be so. This world where my word holds good and my law is always upheld shall not be the whole of existence. The unknown from the known is divided and out of the far unknown the germ of life shall be quickened for which the universe waits. In the age-old order of all things shall the seed of freedom be planted that what shall be, evolve from what is.
YOUNGER SON	What is this new thing freedom?
FATHER	In the far unknown it is hidden where danger is constantly lurking. Out of the risk it shall grow that the World-Father shall bear.
YOUNGER SON	What risk is this?
FATHER	Shall I count what is given you as a heavenly inheritance? Shall I reckon the wealth of worlds

The Prodigal Son

                      with which you shall be endowed?
                      These shall not be counted
                      compared with the risk of my son,
                      who goes he knows not whither
                      to danger he cannot foresee
                      for a purpose he cannot imagine.
                      You yourself are the risk, my child.

YOUNGER SON   Am I not always your son
                      having around me your blessing
                      to keep and protect me?

FATHER   You are bound to a country far off
                      where all that you have and are
                      is staked for an unknown gain.
                      My servants are now at the door
                      bringing the share you inherit
                      from the wealth of the heavens,
                      the share of the younger son.

1st SERVANT   Here is your portion
                      drawn from the wealth of the Moon.

2nd SERVANT   The Moon bequeaths silver
                      to have, to hold and to use.

1st SERVANT   Here is your portion
                      drawn from the wealth of Mercury.

2nd SERVANT   Mercury bequeaths quicksilver
                      to have, to hold and to use.

1st SERVANT   Here is your portion
                      drawn from the wealth of Venus.

2nd SERVANT   Venus bequeaths copper
                      to have, to hold and to use.

1st SERVANT   Here is your portion
                      drawn from the wealth of the Sun.

2nd SERVANT   The Sun bequeaths gold
                      to have, to hold and to use.

1st SERVANT	Here is your portion drawn from the wealth of Mars.
2nd SERVANT	Mars bequeaths iron to have, to hold and to use.
1st SERVANT	Here is your portion drawn from the wealth of Jupiter.
2nd SERVANT	Jupiter bequeaths tin to have, to hold and to use.
1st SERVANT	Here is your portion drawn from the wealth of Saturn.
2nd SERVANT	Saturn bequeaths lead to have, to hold and to use.
SERVANTS (*together*)	Child of the universe endowed with life that flows from starry worlds, within yourself their essences unite into one form. Rich with the wealth of worlds depart to the unknown. Never forget from whence you have your birth. Never forget of whom you are the child.
FATHER (*giving to him a circlet of stars*)	Your head was formed when all the stars in chorus sounded their music. The image of the universe itself is mirrored in its round. This crown of stars I place upon your head, that, in the distant land the star-bred wisdom in your thinking shine.

(*He puts a golden garment on the son.*)

Your heart was forged
out of the fiery Sun,
fired with a golden glow
and set to beat
to the world rhythm.
The golden garment
shall be your clothing
that the Sun-born gold
in your feeling shine.

(*He gives him shoes.*)

Your limbs were shaped
by the power of the Moon
and made in the image
evolved by the stars
of the twelvefold circle
creating together.
Put shoes on your feet
that their forming power
in your willing work.

YOUNGER SON   The strangers whom I meet
will know at sight
that of a worthy house I am the son,
so rich am I with this inheritance.
Now, with your blessing, Father,
I will depart.

(*Another figure, like that of a brother,
appears and stands behind the son. He is
silent.*)

FATHER   The servants shall go
some way along your road.
My son, on a strange adventure
greater than you foresee
you are setting out this day.
To a far country alone
with the risk of everything
you have and are, you go

for a world purpose hid
far beyond your present mind.
My blessing shall be like a cloak
wrapt closely around you.
My love shall be a light
that shines on your distant way.
You are my well loved son,
my fatherhood shall endure
though distance, sin and death
shall come between us both.
Your sonship shall remain
beyond the ages.

YOUNGER SON I shall not forget
to show myself your son.
Farewell, my Father.

FATHER
(*makes a gesture of blessing*)

Farewell my son.

(*The silent brother and the Father look after him as he goes, following the servants, without looking back.*)

SCENE 2

In the far country the son is lying asleep on the ground. A light devil and a dark devil (a luciferic and an ahrimanic being) stand, the first one to the front of the stage, the other to the back.

LIGHT DEVIL There was war in Heaven.
Those who would keep in one
in the great, undivided whole
the will of the gods,
one Godhead, one purpose, one will,
fought with those who had dared
to assert that other will
of selfhood strong in itself
to oppose and convert the plan.

DARK DEVIL There was war in Heaven.

The Prodigal Son

> Those who wielded the might
> of darkness and carried it far
> into the spheres of the light
> with the power of the will against
> them were cast down from the heights,
> dragging with them this other
> whose light shone false
> from his heavenly throne.

LIGHT DEVIL In this country far off
from the realm of God's rule
my power shall work at will.
Where the presence divine
has been withheld
I will shape a world of my own.

DARK DEVIL You dispute this realm with me.
By yourself you soon would dissolve
this world to an airy cloud.
My strength maintains it as real
and fit for us both to work.

LIGHT DEVIL My kingdom shall surely prevail
but I wish not to dwell there alone.
Some creature to be mine own
I desire to entice at my will.

DARK DEVIL It is known that the younger son
has set out from the Father's house
well endowed with his share of its wealth.
Stupid enough he will be
to bend to the purpose I plan,
but you shall entice him first,
since the lust of pride prepares
the heart for the itch of greed.

(A servant appears sent from the Father's house.)

SERVANT You princes who seek below
the realms you have lost above,
hear the message I bring from Him

	whose fatherly care extends from end to end of the world. The younger son is sent out alone from the Father's house to this far country where you without hindrance your will can unfold. He is sent to fulfil in the future a secret purpose divine still unborn from the mind of God. He will not be kept from temptation. The risk is already accepted but in no wise is it intended that he come to serve your will. In this world he shall find the fulfilment of other ends than yours.
LIGHT DEVIL	This world shall be *mine*. The spheres of Heaven are His. Who comes here serves *me*.
SERVANT	Your wisdom may not survey what is still intended. God's will shall still be wrought in this forsaken world.
DARK DEVIL	Let the son come. What is intended can be turned to other uses. Where is he?
SERVANT	He lies here asleep and is dreaming of the home that he left so lately.
LIGHT DEVIL	Poor child, he must certainly waken.
DARK DEVIL	Poor fool, he looks helpless enough.
SERVANT	To return whence I came is my duty. Remember what I have told you. The risk is already taken but his purpose may never be yours.

(*He goes off. The two devils approach the*

sleeping son.)

LIGHT DEVIL   He is here. He must be awakened
to behold the world he inhabits.

DARK DEVIL   He is well endowed. From us shall he learn
to make use of the gifts he brings.

(*At this moment the silent brother comes in and stands on the opposite side of the son to the devils. He remains there until they leave.*)

LIGHT DEVIL   I will give him what he needs
for his new life.

(*He touches the eyes of the son.*)

And when you look,
beautiful and good shall be
what eyes shall see.

(*He waves his arm between the son and the world around. The light devil touches the hands of the son.*)

You will work outwards
from the centre of self.

DARK DEVIL   And when you work,
substantial and real shall be
what hands shall touch.

(*He stamps and makes a gesture of compressing and making firm what is around. The son begins to waken. The dark devil pulls the light devil towards the back of the stage out of sight.*)

DARK DEVIL   Let him learn to enjoy the world
before he learns who rules here.

(*The light devil goes and stands behind the son and opens his arms upwards over him.*)

LIGHT DEVIL	I will give you all the world when you acknowledge me.

(*The dark devil beckons from behind.*)

DARK DEVIL	I will make this world my own and you shall worship me.

(*Both devils disappear and the son wakes up gradually without seeing them. The silent brother leaves too.*)

YOUNGER SON	Where am I? Was it a dream when I thought myself at home in my Father's house? Or am I dreaming now in this strange new world? Which is sleeping? Which is waking?

(*He gets up and begins to look about him.*)

Almost I have forgotten
how I came here.
Once—was it long ago?—
I resolved to leave home
and my Father blessed me
and another stood at his side.
Was it really myself
who wished for that departure?
Why do I not remember
how I came to this place?
Nothing here is familiar.
All is unknown.

(*He goes round looking in all directions with wonder.*)

This is the unknown world I desired
but how strange to be here alone.
I am quite, quite alone.

	Never before was I far from my Father, and servants were always at hand. Now there is none but myself. The unknown creeps up full of dread. Who will answer when I call out in the fear of loneliness?
	(A gnome peeps out.)
GNOME	What makes you sure that you are alone in the world, stupid one? I was peering at your back all the time.
YOUNGER SON	Who are you? Where do you come from?
GNOME	So stupid that you cannot guess. Where have you sprung from, thickheaded one?
YOUNGER SON	From my Father's house.
GNOME	So you are one of the sons, the small one grown bigger. What are you doing here? This is not the place for the sons.
YOUNGER SON	My Father agreed to my going and gave me a share of his wealth.
GNOME	Let us see what you bring.
	(The gnome looks at the shoes and the garment, and begins to show excitement over the crown. But when he sees the metals, he becomes fervent.)
	Grand and glorious is the treasure. Great and generous is the measure that your Father gave.

                Magic mighty
                power portentous
                you shall wield
                in Earth's domain.

YOUNGER SON   What do you mean?
                Is the treasure for use?
                I guarded it safely in awe of my Father.
                That it had use I never knew.

GNOME   Thickheaded one!
(*laughing in scorn*)   They dispatched you here
                without lending the lore
                you would need on the way.

(*A sylph comes hastening past.*)

GNOME   Hie, flibbety gibbet there!
                What did I tell you!
                He is come. He is come.

(*The sylph swerves back again.*)

SYLPH   Are you calling me, wisehead?
                What news have you now?

GNOME   I knew he was coming,
                and now he is here
                but stupid and helpless
                past all belief.

SYLPH   Poor creature, so helpless!
                How lovely his clothing.
                The stars gave his crown,
                the Sun gave his gown,
                the Moon gave his shoes.
                O heavenly creature,
                why be exiled to Earth?

YOUNGER SON   I journeyed here from afar,
                I know not how,
                and have forgotten why.
                Now at least I am not alone.

The Prodigal Son

	Tell me who and what you are.
SYLPH	We nourish, we cherish the increase of the fruit. We lighten, we ripen the seed with the blossom. We hunger, we yearn for the light of the air. We fashion, we form with the forces they bear.
GNOME	We tramp and we tread where the metals are threading their way through the rocks. We pull and we push when the seedlings are growing up out of the ground. We hear and we hold what the heavens are telling in depths of the Earth.
YOUNGER SON	Whom do you serve then?
GNOME AND SYLPH	The Father in Heaven has appointed our place, fashioned our nature and set us our duties. Although we live here in this country afar we still are his servants and know His regard. Since you are His son you also we serve. In willing devotion we take you as lord.
YOUNGER SON	My Father has sent these servants ahead to help me. How great has been His care!
GNOME TO SYLPH	Now he has arrived and intends to remain there is no escape.

SYLPH	How long must I be here when I yearn to be away. The dark always threatens but I flee to the light.

(*She disappears in flight.*)

YOUNGER SON	Why has she gone?
GNOME	We serve as our duty but we long to be free from the world where we feel the forces of matter pressing us hard.
YOUNGER SON	But surely there is much to enjoy here.
GNOME	You have much wealth and far too little sense. I will show you how to use it. You should unite with the Earth the treasure you bring and receive it again to use.

(*An undine comes in with a floating-swimming motion.*)

UNDINE	Has he come? I hear he has come.

(*She encircles the son inspecting him.*)

If only you had not come
we had not needed to stay.

YOUNGER SON	Who are you? Are you also a servant of my Father?
UNDINE	We are swirling and whirling in all that is growing. We are changing, transmuting in all that is living. We seize on the substance that to form is turning and dissolve into process of endless becoming.

YOUNGER SON	What marvellous servants are at work in this world.
UNDINE	The power to transform to dissolve, to refashion shall be yours, if you use it.

(*She goes away as quickly as she came. A salamander appears with great coloured wings.*)

SALAMANDER	The sylphs are saying that the younger son is here.

(*He flies up to the son and gazes at him.*)

Yes, he is here.
By the stars round his head,
by the golden garment
I see he is heaven-sent.

YOUNGER SON	Are you also a servant?
SALAMANDER	We descend from the heights with the life that shall quicken new seeds in the plants. We fashion their forms in the warmth that from Heaven streams down to the Earth. We go up and down from the heights to the depths, from the depths to the heights.
YOUNGER SON	Then you know the way from that world to this?
SALAMANDER	Never forget down here below that you came from above, that you live by favour of Heaven.

(*He flies away again.*)

GNOME	Now come with me, I will show you the wonders of Earth.

	You shall learn how to use
the fortune you bring.
YOUNGER SON	What must I do?
GNOME	The sevenfold treasure
must be laid in the ground
and given to the Earth.
So it will become wealth
for your use and your gain.
You are so stupid,
who can tell how you will waste it!
YOUNGER SON	Already I begin to see with new eyes,
to find wonders with every look.
My Father's house seems like a dream
that fades as I awaken.
This place is my real inheritance
where I shall begin to exist
in the reality for which I yearned.
	(*He and the gnome go off together. The dark devil passes across the back of the stage following them. The light devil comes to the front.*)
LIGHT DEVIL	He has now awakened
and comes into his own.
The world lies before him
to see and enjoy.
We shall share the wealth
that he brings with him,
for we gave him sight
and the lust of enjoyment.
	(*He follows the others.*)

SCENE 3

The gnome pushes on a table and brings bowls. The sylph brings fruit and food and wine.

The Prodigal Son

GNOME
(*grumbling to himself*)

He was stupid from the start
but ignorant more than anything.
He was beginning to learn
and to do what I told him.
But now it's sheer folly!
Oh the waste of it!

SYLPH

Poor creature, so foolish.
How can he forget
that the Sun and the Moon
and the stars in the heavens
have brought forth the riches
that here he is squandering.
What if the Father
should hear of this wasting!

GNOME

When he came
we knew by each feature
that he was the son.
Then they got hold of him
too daft to know them
for what they are.
They made him a wastrel.

SYLPH

And we are the servants
who serve him in sorrow
for he is the son
who with tokens of sonship
came to this country.
My fruits must I offer
as long as they ripen.
With food must I feed him
and serve it in grief.

GNOME (*putting more dishes on the table*)

We are the servants
and must still carry out
the duties of service.
But mark my words,
it cannot go on so for ever.
All is consumed and nothing created.

SYLPH	He is misguided. They also mislead him. How can the Father give him unprotected into their hands?

(*The son comes in with the light and the dark devils as his boon companions.*)

YOUNGER SON	This country is mine for I am the Father's son. The servants knew me at sight. Once it was part of His realm but He comes here no more. He gave me my inheritance and allowed me to depart. At first I hardly knew where I was but now I know my way about. This shall be a kingdom of my own. and I will live from its wealth.
LIGHT DEVIL	It is not yet in reality a kingdom of your own. But you can make it so, if you listen to me.
DARK DEVIL	There is much still to be done to make it a land worth having. If you listen to me, it shall be so.
YOUNGER SON	In the light of this world there emerge to my travelling eye such wonders above and below wherever around me I look. The mountains uplift their heads to the sky spread over the Earth where the great clouds come and go. The moving seas stretch wide their waters from shore to shore and the winds press endlessly on. Within the extent of the land, within the expanse of the seas

are sheltered the manifold wonders
of life that has come into being
in standing stones and resting rocks,
in spreading trees and opening flowers,
in flying birds and gliding fish,
in busy insects and footed beasts.
All things seen are mine to enjoy.

(The gnome comes in still grumbling.)

GNOME This wealth of wonders is kept
and tended by us, the servants,
for you who are idle and thankless.
Without us there would soon be little
still living for you to enjoy.

YOUNGER SON You do the duty appointed
to you within the world order.
It is as it should be.
You maintain and I enjoy.

LIGHT DEVIL When you looking see
and seeing know yourself
and the world outspread around,
that use of sense you have from me.

DARK DEVIL When you handling touch
and touching know to be
what is about you firm and true
you have reality from me.

YOUNGER SON Do I not possess the world
out of myself?
Am I not rich with my own treasure?

BOTH DEVILS You are in debt to us!

YOUNGER SON I was so rich being my Father's son
and now I am in debt.
How can this be?

LIGHT DEVIL Your golden cloak shall be mine.
You owe it to me.

(He takes the cloak, leaving the son with only the golden stole.)

DARK DEVIL You owe me the stars in your crown.
I shall make good use of them.

(He takes some of the stars, but they will not all come off in his hands.)

YOUNGER SON What has become of me?
You have taken what is mine
and left me less than I was.
Take back what I have from you
and give me my own.

LIGHT DEVIL You cannot have what you have lost.
But see, I will comfort you.
You shall have a cloak from me.

(He puts a reddish glittering cloak round the son's shoulders and embraces him.)

You shall be my dearest brother,
and share my kingdom with me.

YOUNGER SON *(puzzled)* Am I to find new brothers?

DARK DEVIL I can use your stars better than you
but you shall have something from me.

(He puts some paper stars in place of the gold ones.)

You think paper is too poor?
Look at what is printed there.
You are getting some of my secrets.

(He takes him by the arm and hisses in his ear.)

You will be my crony one day,
if you know how to make good.
His kingdom is in the clouds.

The Prodigal Son

You will get something solid with me.

(*The son looks frightened and draws away.*)

YOUNGER SON
(*looking down at himself*)
How different I look,
but I am not the son in my Father's
  house.
Here I must learn to change
and be something on my own.

(*The sylph comes in with a big dish. When she sees the son she screams and puts the dish down.*)

SYLPH
Oh fearful misery,
what has befallen you?

YOUNGER SON (*angry*)
Stop wailing, bring the food.
My friends and I are ready for the feast.

(*The gnome comes in.*)

GNOME
What is this all about?
Glory be! What have you come to?

SYLPH
I shall be off, away,
this is no lord for me.

GNOME
Stop, we may not forget
what has been laid on us
as our duty.
This world must be maintained
as long as lasts the strength
with which we do our work.

SYLPH
Since he came, what has he given
to us of the wealth he brought?
He fritters it away himself.
Look at him now. What hope is there
for him in time to come?

GNOME
What was appointed to us
must be continued.

(*He and the sylph finish setting the table*

and retire.)

YOUNGER SON   Take your seats my friends.

(*They all sit at the table.*)

The servants know their work.
What they expect from me
I never comprehend.
This world around us
gives what we can enjoy.
The experience of all it gives
is ample occupation.
It fills my soul to the brim.

LIGHT DEVIL   Fill yourself to the brim
with the wealth of this world.
In what is around and within
you will discover enough
to swell out your inner being
with the warm content of feeling
that fosters the glow of selfhood.
You will feel yourself right and good,
indulging in sympathy
with all that is filled with beauty.
But be warned.
If into this world you descend
beyond the stage of experience
you will forfeit your happiness.
You will be drawn to the interest
of what is belonging to matter.
In getting and spending,
your human nature will coarsen
and your soul that would upwards soar
will downwards sink to the depths.
Fill yourself full with all
that will enrich your selfhood,
but don't be involved with this world.
I will lead you upward and onward.

DARK DEVIL   Don't listen too much to him.

                    He is on bad terms with reality
                    and wants to lure you away.
                    There is more to know in this world
                    than you have discovered already.
                    I can show you the secret
                    of how to calculate forces
                    that work below the appearance.
                    What you grasp, you can control.
                    You can become the master
                    of its mighty mechanism
                    and steer the power of this world
                    to the ends you set yourself.
                    None can be your teacher but me.
                    Wake up from your childish state
                    and learn the powers of your mind.
                    With them control the world
                    and make it a place of your own.
                    Descend with me into reality
                    and become the master.

YOUNGER SON   I met you both first in this country
(looking from one   and both have become my companions
to the other)   but each contradicts the other
                    and offers the opposite counsel,
                    and here am I between you both.
                    What shall I do?

LIGHT DEVIL   Follow me to the heights
                    where the darkness fades
                    and dissolves in the distance.
                    The burden of your existence
                    shall fall away from you.

DARK DEVIL   Come with me to the depths
                    where you shall know the darkness
                    and master its powers.
                    You shall triumph over existence
                    and steer its course yourself.

YOUNGER SON   You confuse me until
                    I cannot tell what to believe.

LIGHT DEVIL	Your pride will make you incline to me.
DARK DEVIL	Your greed will pull you towards me.
YOUNGER SON	What I have now is enough. Here is feasting in plenty. Eat and be merry with me.

(*The light devil takes wine, the dark devil food, the son both.*)

DARK DEVIL	Eat and feed the brain that the brain breed mind and mind masters all things.
LIGHT DEVIL	Forget him and turn to me. Drink till the winged soul soars free from solid flesh.
YOUNGER SON	Eating and drinking, tasting and feasting from all the fruits of this land there is that lacking that never before was missing. A new hunger is in me.
DARK DEVIL	Eat more.
YOUNGER SON	I cannot live by this bread only. From what did I live before?
LIGHT DEVIL	You start to hunger for the spirit.
DARK DEVIL	We must have more food. The dishes are empty. Where are the servants?
YOUNGER SON (*to light devil*)	Am I craving for the spirit?
DARK DEVIL	Spirit is empty shadow, an abstraction. You cannot feed on that. Send the servants for real food.

(*The gnome and the sylph appear, carrying*

The Prodigal Son

empty dishes, baskets.)

DARK DEVIL Provide quickly.
(*to them*)
(*The gnome shakes his head; the sylph wails.*)

SYLPH No more, no more is there to bring.
Our strength is failing,
the blossoms are fading,
the fruit is falling,
the harvest has withered away.

GNOME Our duty was done
while our strength has lasted,
but now we are starved ourselves.
All was consumed, nothing created
and famine follows.

YOUNGER SON But where is the wealth
you put to use for me?
What has become of my inheritance?
I must be provided for.

GNOME Wasted, all is wasted
that you brought with you.
You have taken all and given nothing
till the servants no longer
have power to provide.
Now we must leave you, thankless one,
to hunger and want.

YOUNGER SON What does he mean?
What shall I do now?

LIGHT DEVIL So this is the end to joy and feasting
that promised so well at the beginning.
You should have listened sooner to me.

(*He goes away.*)

DARK DEVIL Hunger and want are things I can use.
You have no choice. You must serve me.
I will show you now where you belong.

(*He beckons and calls. Some pigs come in.*)

Stay here and herd pigs.

YOUNGER SON There is no choice. What could I
otherwise do?

DARK DEVIL That fantastic brother of mine
wanted to make you a god
after his own image.
You will find your place with me,
when you learn the power of the beast
and conjure it up in yourself.

(*He goes away.*)

(*The son sits dejectedly by the pigs. He takes off the cloak that the devil gave him and folds it up to sit on.*)

PIGS We grub in the ground,
we rout out the roots,
we lave in the mud,
we hog up the husks.
We are exiles on Earth,
disguised in our kind
from the creatures we are
in our heavenly shape.
But in eating we still
make magic divine,
digesting base food
into forces of life.

YOUNGER SON You are my companions now.
May I eat with you?
I am famished with hunger.

PIGS Eat with us, if you are able.

(*They push husks towards him. Bending down to take them his crown falls off and he tears the last portion of his golden garment. A pig eats the paper off the crown. He tries to eat, but throws the husks away.*)

YOUNGER SON   It is useless.
The food that the pigs can take
is empty and coarse to me.
The magic that they command
is unknown to me.
I cannot be as they.

(*He sits down with his head in his hands in despair. The silent brother comes and stands behind him.*)

YOUNGER SON   Who am I?
(*to himself*)
What am I doing here?
What I had was not my own
but lent to me by my Father
and that has been lost.
I am reduced to what I am myself
and I am left quite alone
in a land that is not my home.
I know now what I am myself.
But what shall become of me?

(*He pauses and then continues.*)

I can recall to mind
how it is in my Father's house
under wise and loving rule.
The servants come and go
each with his duty content,
each with the bread he needs
for sustenance and life.
There is bread enough and to spare
while here I starve for food.
What the servants have and leave
would save me from perishing.

(*He pauses again. The pigs gather round but he does not notice them.*)

Once I have been the son

	with his place in the Father's house. But that can never be now since my heritage is lost. I left my house as a son, as a servant I will return and will say at once to my Father I am unworthy of sonship but take me into your service. Make me one of your servants for I cannot live without food that will feed me with spirit-life.
PIGS (*in excitement*)	Will you go back to the Father's house? Take us with you. We also come from there and are exiles here.
YOUNGER SON	I cannot remember the way by which I was brought here. Now I must find the road alone, with what strength I have. It cannot fail to be hard, lonely and full of danger. How can I take others along when I may fail myself?
PIGS	Do not forget us when you come home. Come back and fetch us again to the place, where we should be. Remember us.
YOUNGER SON	You have been my companions here and I will not forget you. Farewell till some happier time. I arise and go to my Father on a road unknown and long, not as a son but a beggar, myself for what I am. As a son I died in this country. Shall I live again as a servant?

(*The silent brother follows him out.*)

SCENE 4

The son comes along wearily but firmly.

YOUNGER SON Hard and steep is the road.
Sometimes I see in the distance,
shining from far beyond,
the light of my Father's house.
More often I lose altogether
sight of what lies ahead
and the weariness of the moment
smothers the sense of my purpose.
But somewhere within me
steadfastly shines the flame,
the resolve that was lit in the hour
when in sheer desolation
I came to myself.

(The figure of the silent brother appears and passes in front of him onwards. From the side, the light devil comes to meet him.)

LIGHT DEVIL You have left the far country behind
and have taken a course of your own.
Where are you going?

YOUNGER SON To the Father's house.

LIGHT DEVIL In what poor shape you will appear.
You departed proud as a prince,
with a goodly inheritance,
into a world that offered
its fill of experience.
Outside your Father's rule
you could freely find yourself
and become by right the master
in a world of your own.
Will you creep back a beggar?

YOUNGER SON	I have resolved to beg my Father to make me into a servant.
LIGHT DEVIL	A poor ending to a noble beginning! You are worth a better fate. You can become a prince in my world if you will acknowledge me.
YOUNGER SON	My place shall be in the Father's world. My service and my love I offer to Him, For I have grievously sinned against Him.
LIGHT DEVIL	So you refuse my over-generous help! But what of the gifts you had of me? Who will repay what belongs to me?
YOUNGER SON	They cannot be restored to you. Without them I could not make my way now. But they have been changed in use and transformed from what they were. One day you will find them anew when you seek what is yours in my Father's house.
LIGHT DEVIL	Shall I be admitted there again, I who fell from my place?
YOUNGER SON	When I see to the end of the road, the light that beckons to me is warm with grace.
LIGHT DEVIL	When you come there, remember me. (*He goes away. The dark devil appears from behind.*)
DARK DEVIL (*with a sneer*)	So you are escaping at last, a refugee from a world where you failed. You lost a lot on this venture with nothing to show at the end. You should have heeded me and things would have turned out much

	better for you. But it is still not too late. I will make you a last offer. Take service with me and you shall inhabit a world where everything is at your disposal; where your will shall be the measure of all things.
YOUNGER SON	In your world I should lose myself. On the way to the Father's house I find myself.
DARK DEVIL	But you are not what you are without me. Look what I gave you.
YOUNGER SON	You gave me what I cannot do without. But what you give is not the same as when you gave it.
DARK DEVIL	You are robbing me.
YOUNGER SON	If I am redeemed, your gifts will be redeemed in me.
DARK DEVIL (*speaking in pain*)	I am condemned to my own realm and how shall I be released?

(*He goes away. The son begins to walk on, comforting himself with a psalm, e.g. 'I will lift up mine eyes to the hills'. He goes off and from the other side appears one of the servants of the Father on the look-out.*)

SERVANT	Again today He bade me go out and look into the distance. Whom does He expect? Can He hope that one who was lost will return again home?

(*The Father appears, also looking out.*)

SERVANT	There is no one in sight, sire.

FATHER	My eyes may see further than yours.
SERVANT	Do you expect him, sire, who went so long ago?
FATHER	It is more than time he came. He must find the road hard to be so slow coming.
SERVANT	Shall some of us go to his aid?
FATHER	That may not be. A great helper is with him who will speak to him with his own voice from within. In selfhood he shall return. But the way is filled with dangers and the risk will not be surmounted until he comes within sight.

(*They both look out.*)

Return to the house.
Call the servants together in haste.
He is coming.

(*The servant goes away. The Father moves forward and holds out his arms.*)

My son, my lost son,
the one who departed and comes again,
whose life was risked and yet lives.

(*The son comes in, the silent brother behind him.*)

The road was long and anxious,
it has cost you so much, my son,
that you can hardly step to the door.
The life of your youth is exhausted
in the struggle to make the way
back from the country afar
to the place where the Father dwells.

The Prodigal Son

My heart overflows with compassion
to see how the pain and the labour,
the fear and the loneliness
have put their marks upon you.

(*He embraces his son.*)

Out of the shadow of death you come
back to life.
Out of the place where you were lost
into the arms of the Father.

(*The son embraces him now.*)

YOUNGER SON   My Father, unworthy am I
to be called again your son.
Unworthy am I to speak
with the name of Father to you.
So damaged am I by sin
who against Heaven itself
have sinned in the selfish wasting
of the manifold gifts of the Spirit
you gave me in fatherly care.
In your eyes and before your judgment
I have sinned against the Spirit
and spoilt the shape of my sonhood.
O Father, I am not worthy
to be called again your son.

FATHER
(*to the two servants
who have returned*)   Call the servants together in haste;
there is much now to be done.
Fetch out the robe, the best,
the one that was laid away
for the hour of our greatest joy.

(*The servants go and return with the robe.*)

SON (*to Father*)   Let them bring the clothes of a servant;
I dare not ask for more.

SERVANTS
(*offering it to the
son*)   We bring you the precious robe
woven of golden sunlight,
threaded with silver moonbeams,

                crossed with the copper of Venus,
                fluent with Mercury's motion,
                strong with the iron of Mars,
                glinting with Jupiter's tin,
                weighted with Saturn's lead,
                made by the great ones in chorus
                who each in his moving sphere
                brings forth the wealth of the heavens.
                Long ago it was fashioned but never
                has he been found who should wear it.

                (*They put it on the son.*)

YOUNGER SON   A garment my Father gave me
                when I set out from his house
                into that country afar.
                By my own sin I lost it,
                the robe of my Father's son.
                Shall I, become unworthy
                to be called again his son,
                inherit a robe more precious,
                more princely still than the first?

FATHER   Bring now the ring for his finger
(*to servants*)   that never yet has been worn.
                Bring for his feet the new sandals
                in which he shall walk in my realm.

YOUNGER SON   None of these gifts are deserved
(*to Father*)   that out of compassion you give.

                (*Servants bring in from one side the ring,
                from the other the sandals and put them on
                him.*)

SERVANTS   We bring you the sacred ring,
                the sign of the ultimate whole.
                Through one it embraces all,
                embracing all it is one.
                The universe gave it shape,
                the Sun gave substance of gold.
                The power divine within it

shall be held in your hand.

(*They put it on his finger.*)

We bring you sandals unworn
that you go with kingly step
into your Father's domain
where you shall be son and heir.
The gods who work from below
have fashioned them for your feet
to give you the gift of strength
from their world-upholding might.

(*They put the sandals on his feet.*)

YOUNGER SON   How can this be?
The touch of the starry robe
quickens my soul to life.
The might that flows through the ring
restores me back to my self.
The power of the shoes on my feet
gives me the courage again
to enter the Father's house.
How can I, a wastrel lost,
receive the vesture of healing
which the elder son himself
was not appointed to wear?
What does this mean?

FATHER   My son, you were lost and are found.
Your garment was spoilt and torn.
The circlet upon your head
was broken, the shoes worn out.
Now you return in need
of the forces of Heaven to heal
and renew your strength.
But from the venture you bring
one achievement wrought by yourself
out of the spirit within.
In despair you awoke to selfhood
and by its power alone

                you made the perilous way
                back to the house of your Father.
                You bring what is here unknown,
                freedom, true virtue of selfhood,
                which none of the sons of God
                but only he, who went out
                alone to the country afar
                and ventured all that he had,
                could offer up to the heavens;
                the new force of life they need
                but cannot themselves bring forth.
                In the far country of Earth
                the power of the future was born
                when man to freedom awakes.
                You were lost and are found again
                bringing the seed to selfhood.

YOUNGER SON   I saw myself as a beggar,
                not as one with a treasure to give.
                I knew myself to be starving
                for lack of the heavenly bread.
                So I came to beg.

FATHER   The beginning of freedom
                is loneliness and desolation.
                The struggle for freedom
                is the awakening of the self to itself.
                The harvest of freedom
                is love that seeks beyond itself.
                The end of freedom
                is resurrection for the world.

YOUNGER SON   I never knew that I set out for such an end.

FATHER   Not for yourself alone, did you go.
                The risk on himself the Father took
                for a greater end than you could foresee.
                To the shadow of death he sent the son
                who now is born again to life.
                For which great rejoicing shall be made

through all this house.

(*To the servants.*)

Make ready the feast.
Bring the best in abundance.
The fatted calf shall be killed today.
Voices shall sing and feet shall dance
and music be made for all our joy.
Call those of my household
to share the feast.
Let them come to rejoice
with me for my son,
for him who was lost and is found at last,
for him who was dead and returns to life.
Let him be placed
at the head of the feast
who ventured alone to the world
    unknown
and brought back the treasure
he went to seek.

(*The servants lead the son to the doors of the house and there appears the silent brother standing there to receive him. They all go in, the Father last. Music is heard from the background. This could be the singing of a psalm or other suitable music. A servant or servants could do Eurythmy or dancing outside the portico. The elder son comes in.*)

ELDER SON   All in the fields is in order
over the stretch of lands
where I went as my Father's regent
to help with the husbandry
and remained until now.
My Father will welcome the news
of a promising harvest to come.

(*A servant comes out.*)

What is astir in the house?

	Music? Dancing? Why then?
	(*To the servant.*)
	What is this sound of music and of feasting within the house?
SERVANT	Today, sire, while you were gone to the distant fields, your brother who went from home to a far-off country was seen slowly approaching this place. I saw him and would not have known, so wasted and weary was he, that he was the younger son. But your Father knew him at sight and ran in compassion to meet him.
ELDER SON	My younger brother is here? Returning in such poor shape?
SERVANT	I heard him say of himself that all his wealth was lost and he an unworthy son. But the Father gave him the robe that no one yet had worn and he ordered the calf to be killed, the best of the fatlings we had. A splendid feast is here. Come in, sire, and share the joy that your Father has in the son who has come back safe and sound.
ELDER SON	You say he has wasted all of the wealth he took away?
SERVANT	He came like a beggar home but full of regret and grief.
ELDER SON	And for him the fatted calf? No, I will not come in. Go back to the feast and say I remain outside.

(He sits down. The servant goes and soon the Father comes out.)

FATHER My son, your brother is come,
he whom we mourned as lost.
He came by a weary road
and struggled sore on the way.
Come in and bid him welcome.

ELDER SON Has he not utterly wasted
the inheritance you gave?
Shall I welcome a wastrel?

FATHER Think how he has travelled alone
in the place of strange temptation
where the princes of evil work.
Come and rejoice with us
that he himself is saved.
Your place at the feast is empty.

ELDER SON For him you killed the fatted calf,
for the one who wasted your wealth
and spent his all with companions,
spendthrift and frivolous.
But I, who have served you truly
and observed your rule and order
faithfully day by day,
have never been given a feast
to which I could call my friends.
Not so much as a kid was slain for me
to provide a feast in my honour;
but for him, the fatted calf was killed,
the best that we had.

FATHER My son, you are always with me,
at my side or taking my place
on your journeys through our lands.
All that I have is likewise your own.
We are one without separation,
in mind, in heart and in will,
having all purpose in common.

But your brother from us was divided,
and walked in the ways of error
in the land beset with evil
till the shadow of death was on him.
We should give our best for the feasting
and rejoice with all our folk,
for your brother was lost and is found,
was dead and is risen to life.

(*In the portico appear the younger son and the silent brother. The younger son stays there. The silent brother walks across to the elder brother and holds out his hand.*)

SILENT BROTHER
Our brother was dead and is alive again, was lost and is found.

(*He leads him across to the side of the younger son.*)

FATHER
For my son was dead and is alive again, was lost and is found.

(*The music is heard again and they go into the house.*)

EVELYN FRANCIS CAPEL
Celebrating Festivals Around the World

The Christian festivals have come to be closely connected with the yearly seasonal cycle of the northern countries. This poses a question: Should the festivals be tied to nature's yearly cycle or should the Christian year be a common experience all over the world?

Evelyn Capel addresses this problem by delving into what lies behind the rhythms of the natural year, describing the parts played by the Archangels and the elemental beings, and showing that the festivals are continuing events. Their purpose is to show humanity that the spirit of man is of heavenly origin, and their celebration is part of the conversation between the heavens and humanity.

The author provides practical advice and suggestions, and five delightful and instructive plays.

144pp; 23.5 × 15.5 cm; sewn softback; £7.95; ISBN 0 904693 29 5

EVELYN FRANCIS CAPEL
Understanding Death

As human beings on earth we all inevitably face death. But should we allow ourselves to feel fear when confronted with this reality?

Understanding Death is a lucid guide to an undoubtedly difficult subject. Evelyn Capel shows how we can begin to comprehend the true meaning of our physical incarnation on this earth by looking at the spiritual background to life and death. She offers practical advice on caring for the dying in a straightforward and easily digestible way—for those who will need the information immediately. Her tone throughout is clear and unsentimental, but always retains a profound compassion for those suffering grief.

48pp; 210 × 135 mm; paperback; £3.95; ISBN 0 904693 27 9

EVELYN FRANCIS CAPEL
An Introduction to Counselling from a Spiritual Perspective

'... It is of the greatest importance that the counsellor can discard his own prejudices, the good as well as the bad, and transcend his personal standards of judgement. This is necessary, because in spiritual reality it is not he who is the counsellor, but the higher spiritual being of the other person, who should be allowed to speak through the one who gives counsel.'

In introducing a spiritual perspective to the art of counselling, Evelyn Capel extends the limits of contemporary psychological thinking.

64pp; 210 × 135 mm; paperback; £4.95; ISBN 0 904693 19 8

EVELYN FRANCIS CAPEL & ALFRED DOWUONA-HAMMOND

Christ in the Old and New Testaments
Towards a New Theology

'... *Those around Jesus Christ were accustomed to rely on the standard set by the law. He who did not offend against the law would be saved from sinning. But He put another picture before them. He spoke of the human soul so filled with enthusiasm for what it could become by the power of the Spirit within, that it would be greater than the one that was only able to keep regulations.*'

A powerful account of the life of Christ on Heaven and Earth and a radical reassessment of traditional theology.

182pp; 210 × 135 mm; paperback; £6.95; ISBN 0 904693 21 X

EVELYN FRANCIS CAPEL
Pictures from the Apocalypse

'... *And I saw an angel come down from heaven, having the key of the bottomless pit and a great chain in his hand. And he laid hold on the dragon, that old serpent, which is the Devil, and Satan, and bound him a thousand years. And cast him into the bottomless pit, and shut him up, and set a seal upon him, that he should deceive the nations no more, till the thousand years should be fulfilled: and after that he must be loosed a season ...*'

— from the Revelation of St John

To understand St John's Revelation today, argues Evelyn Capel, it is necessary to extend one's comprehension to include the heavenly. The Apocalypse presents vast sweeps of history in a series of pictorial imaginations. These 'imaginations' are not intended to be understood by intellectual explanations, but by 'the ability to form pictures in one's own mind and to let them unfold themselves in one's thinking ...'

122pp; 210 × 135 mm; paperback; £5.95; ISBN 0 904693 18 X